Straw Bale Construction Manual

Gernot Minke · Benjamin Krick

Straw Bale Construction Manual

Design and Technology of a Sustainable Architecture

Birkhäuser · Basel

Table of contents

II Built examples in detail

Preface

New developments, new research results, new production methods and new structural applications afforded a complete rewriting of the book *Building with Straw* by Gernot Minke and Friedemann Mahlke that was published in 2005. Especially prefabrication of wall and roof elements, new solutions for loadbearing vault and dome structures and new data for fire resistance, heat conductivity, CO_2 content and primary energy content were added. To this new publication, Benjamin Krick contributed as co-author.

This book is based on the German edition *Handbuch Strohballenbau,* published in 2014 by ökobuch Verlag. For this English edition, nine recently completed case studies from all over the world have been selected and added.

We would like to extend our thanks to all who sent us material of new research results and projects. We are grateful that we could use the drawings which Friedemann Mahlke made for the first book and our special thanks go to Ria Stein from Birkhäuser, who was responsible for the copy-editing, project management and also helped with the translation.

Gernot Minke and Benjamin Krick
March 2020

I The technology of straw bale building

1 Introduction

Purpose and objectives of this book

Straw bale building has been experiencing a veritable boom since the 1990s, which first emanated from the USA – here, in fact, an increase in activities showed itself as early as the 1970s – and then spread to Canada and Australia. The renewed interest in straw bale construction also inspired and spurred on those who had been experimenting in this field in Europe, and it is gradually reaching Asia and South America as well.

The idea to use straw as a building material and the know-how of the various techniques that are being used left the ecological domain a long time ago. Increasingly, international and national networks and symposia on this topic are also attracting mainstream architects and engineers. Various examples of completed buildings, among them private residences as well as commercial, educational and cultural buildings, prove the point that straw bale building offers a fresh and highly promising outlook – both from an environmental and an economical perspective.

In contrast to most publications on straw bale building in the past, this book explains in great detail the structural and physical aspects and problems of this building technique. It gives planners and builders – be they architects, engineers, craftsmen or laymen – an idea of the building-physical and structural basics and particularities of straw

bale building and highlights potential faults that may lead to avoidable damages. The pictured projects from different countries and climatic zones emphasise the great variety of applications and designs of straw bale building and present this building technique as a sustainable, inexpensive alternative to conventional building methods.

About the contents

The *first chapter* of the book highlights the advantages and disadvantages of straw bale building, particularly with a view to the now common demand for sustainability. It also relates to second thoughts and anxieties of potential users. The *second chapter* contains a brief account of the history of straw bale building and its current state of proliferation. The *third chapter* gives an introduction on the structural and physical properties of straw as building material and straw bales as building elements. *Chapters 4 and 5* describe the important issues of thermal insulation, fire protection, moisture protection, sound insulation and the primary energy content of straw. *Chapters 6 to 10* explain the structural behaviour of straw, the different wall construction systems with their respective pros and cons and they elaborate on the possibilities of insulating roofs and floors with straw bales. *Chapter 11* documents the assembly process in detail, including schematic drawings of all important structural details. Next, *chapter 12* draws attention to the various options of weatherproofing and finishing of walls. *Chapters 13 and 14* look at cost and time planning and give advice on how faults can be avoided. Finally, *part II* closes with an assorted selection of modern straw bale houses from all over the world. The book's appendix contains references to related publications and a subject index.

Building with straw – a contribution to sustainability in construction

Straw is a renewable building material that will grow again every year. It is a ubiquitous resource that is naturally recyclable and does not pose any problems in terms of its disposal: in the event of building demolition it can be easily separated from other materials and – for instance – can be used as mulch in the garden or in agriculture for the decompacting of soil. The production of straw bales and transport to the building site consume relatively little energy compared to other building materials; thus, this construction method has hardly any negative impact on the environment. The production of straw bales consumes approx. 14 MJ/m³ of energy – as opposed to mineral wool, which requires 1077 MJ/m³ for its production, 77 times more than straw. Moreover, the production of straw bales for 1 m² wall construction with a U-value of 0.15 W/(m²·K) some 3 kWh energy are needed (Krick 2008), compared to approx. 100 kWh if the wall insulation consists of polystyrene panels *(1.3)* The chemical absorption of carbon dioxide during photosynthesis is proportionally even higher than the carbon dioxide emissions caused by the production and transport of straw bales. Buildings with thermal insulation made of straw can, therefore, help to substantially reduce carbon dioxide emissions in the construction industry. Consequently, straw meets all the requirements of a "sustainable" building material, even more so than wood since the production and processing of timber require much more energy and produce much more carbon dioxide than the production of straw bales from straw.

1.1

1.2

1.1 Three-storey passive house with straw bales and timber in Kurtatsch, South Tyrol, Italy, 2003 (Design: Margareta Schwarz, Werner Schmidt)

1.2 Two-storey Spiral House with loadbearing external walls, Co. Mayo, Ireland, 2003 (Design: Norita Clesham)

1.3 Comparison of primary energy demand for the production of various insulation materials for 1 m² wall construction in a passive house

Further advantages of straw bale building

Official building tests on straw bale walls conducted in Germany and Austria produced the following results:
– fire resistance rating of F90
– material designation: normally inflammable
– coefficient of heat conductivity:
  $\lambda_R = 0.0456 \, W/mK$

This means, that straw bale insulated wall structures can be used for all one- and two-storey buildings, no matter whether they are single-family or duplex homes, terrace houses, garages, agricultural buildings, childcare centres, schools, hospitals or office buildings. Under certain conditions, multi-storey buildings can be also permissible. Straw bale insulated houses can achieve passive-house standards. Passive houses are buildings with an annual heating energy consumption of less than $15 \, kWh/m^2$. In such buildings the installation of a conventional heating system is not economical as the heating cost is lower than the standing charge for a gas connection, possibly even lower than the cost for the operation of the circulation pump of a conventional heating system.

In Germany's agricultural production, for instance, straw is available in large quantities. According to research undertaken by the authors, the straw harvest of only one year would theoretically provide sufficient insulation material for 700,000 single-family homes. The long lifespan of straw bale buildings is proven by numerous examples from the United States. The oldest still inhabited house is approx. 100 years old (see chapter 2).
Straw bales are ideal for do-it-yourself construction: the advantages do not only encompass building-cost savings, but also the social interaction of the participants of the building process. Family members, neighbours and friends that are usually excluded from the building process can

participate. This creates a strong sense of identity for the clients and possibly their children with their own house, their "own four walls". For all participants, the act of the house building is an exciting interactive and gratifying social experience (1.4–1.6). In the USA, Canada and Australia, the future house owners will frequently host so-called "work parties" to raise the straw bale walls, inviting friends and family and even strangers to join them.

Objections and anxieties

Frequently, one stumbles across substantial doubts and subliminal anxiety when people are confronted with the idea of living or working in houses with walls made of straw bales. These reactions are mainly due to a lack of knowledge and an irrational fear of the new and unknown. This book will try to face the lack of knowledge by enlightening the reader through competent information; the mentioned anxiety can only be dispersed by means of rational arguments – another task this book will attempt to tackle. In the USA, research has repeatedly addressed the issue of whether insects, mice or even rats lived in historical straw bale buildings – which was, however, not the case.

Fire hazard
No one would deny the fact that loose straw easily catches fire; however, the reality that straw bale walls that are rendered on both sides achieve a fire resistance of 90 minutes (F90 rating) is still widely unknown. This was first established according to Austrian building standards (see chapter 4) and has meanwhile also been verified in Germany.

A nesting site for mice
Neither mice nor other rodents feed on straw. However, straw can provide an attractive nesting ground for them. Just as it is the case with any other ventilated exterior cladding and insulation material, mice must be prevented from

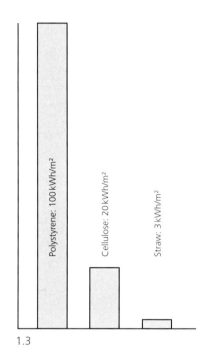

1.3

entering the wall construction and finding cavities there. Plaster or meshes provide adequate protection against rodents. In a straw bale test building at Swarthmore College (1994–1998) that was dismantled after four years and where every single straw bale was examined, no evidence of the existence of vermin could be found.

Termites

Evidently, straw is not a feast for termites either. Some species may be able to digest straw, but they clearly prefer wood as food. Steen et al. report that doors and window frames of a historical straw bale house were infested – the straw itself, however, remained intact (Steen et al. 1994, page 64).

Moulds

The fear that moulds might develop on straw bales is unfounded – provided the correct construction rules are observed; moulds cannot develop on dry straw. The correct construction rules involve the use of dry straw bales; that means that their moisture content is lower than 15 %, and that either a vapour barrier is installed on the inside surface to prevent moisture from entering the bales or that the exterior finish is vapour-permeable enough so that potential condensate can diffuse out. Whether or not a wall build-up complies with these requirements can be established by means of officially authorised methods of calculation (see chapter 4).

During plastering, it has to be made sure that the plaster dries out relatively fast. For this, the plaster must allow sufficient diffusion so that the straw, which has become moist during plastering, can dry out quickly. If the earth plaster contains too many organic aggregates such as sawdust or straw chaff, it will dry out very slowly, which facilitates the formation of moulds. Hence, builders have to make sure – especially when the plaster layers are thick – that the earlier layers dry out before the last layer is applied. Furthermore, the last layer should contain no – or at least very few – organic additives.

Dust allergies

As a result of the building process, people with dust allergies may be affected and face unpleasant consequences. Allergic persons should therefore wear a breathing protection mask as a precaution. Occupants of a completed building with rendered walls will not face any risk.

1.4

1.5

1.6

1.4–1.6 "Green classroom" at the State Horticultural Show 2006 in Wernigerode, Germany. Here, loadbearing straw bale walls were built by laypersons under the direction of architect Friederike Fuchs.

2 History and proliferation of straw bale building

2.1

Early buildings (1880–1980)

The beginning of the history of straw bale building coincides with the appearance of straw bale presses in the USA in the 19th century: between 1861 and 1865 hay was pressed into bales to facilitate feeding of war horses in the Civil War; in 1872, a press driven by horse power is mentioned, by 1884, there were steam-driven presses. The first recorded straw bale buildings were erected in sparsely wooded Nebraska. Probably they were initially built as temporary shelters for farm workers but soon people noticed their durability and the comfort they provided. By 1886, a school with a single classroom had been built near Bayard in Nebraska's Scotts Bluff County

(Steen et al. 1994). These early straw bale buildings were constructed without timber substructure, with the straw bale walls directly supporting the roof. In the literature, this "loadbearing" construction method was later referred to as "Nebraska technique".

The oldest remaining straw bale buildings erected with the loadbearing method that are still inhabited were built between 1900 and 1914 and were extended in 1940 (2.1). The Nebraska technique had its heyday between 1915 and 1930 (2.2); Welsch (1970) mentions approx. 70 buildings from this period, 13 of which still existed in 1993. A church with loadbearing straw bale walls, the Pilgrim Holiness

2.1 Martin Monhart House, Arthur, Nebraska, USA, 1925

2.2 Fawn Lake Ranch, Hyannis, Nebraska, USA, 1900–1914

2.2

2.3

2.4

2.5

2.6

2.3 Pilgrim Holiness Church, Arthur, Nebraska, USA, 1928

2.4 Burrit Mansion, Huntsville, Alabama, USA, 1938

2.5 Maison Feuillette, Montargis, France, 1921

2.6 Country house, Heeze, the Netherlands, 1944 (Design: Jan Gubbels)

2.7 The oldest straw bale building in Norway was built in 1956 with loadbearing straw bale walls.

2.8 Biohaus Hennef-Süchterscheid, Germany, 1979 (Design: Rudolf Doernach)

2.9 Cover of The Last Straw journal

2.7

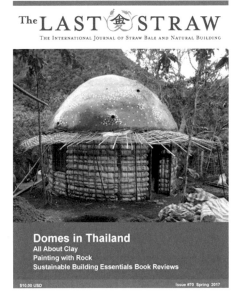

2.9

Church, was built in Arthur, Nebraska, in 1928 (2.3). Burrit Mansion in Huntsville, Alabama (2.4), was built in 1938 and is probably one of the first wooden two-storey post-and-beam structures with straw bale infill panels in the USA; it contains 2200 straw bales as part of its walls, ceilings and roof. Today, it is a museum. At the end of the Great Depression and as a consequence of industrialisation of the construction process in the mid-1930s, building with straw bales became marginalised.

In Europe, a number of straw bale houses were built as well. Probably the oldest known straw bale building of Europe is Maison Feuillette, built in 1921 in Montargis, France. This two-storey house of 100 m² is a timber post-and-beam construction with straw bale infill (2.5). In the Netherlands, a house in Heeze (2.6) dates back to 1944 (Steen et al. 1994). Even before modern straw bale building became successful in the USA during the 1980s and a long time before it reached Europe, the German architect Rudolf Doernach built a wooden post-and-beam structure consisting of round timber posts and straw bale insulated walls in Hennef-Süchterscheid in 1979 (2.8). However, the building did not receive wide attention

and remained widely unknown to the international alternative building community. Possibly, that was due to the fact that the building was based on a somewhat immature design: bales were not plastered but covered only by a rough exterior timber cladding. In order to achieve wind-tightness, the bales were covered with foil on the outside. That, however, obstructed vapour diffusion – thus leading to partial decay. Consequently, the bales had to be removed a few years later and were replaced with a conventional wall build-up.

The renaissance of straw bale buildings

The development in the USA
The 1970s and 1980s produced a fair number of publications on the topic in the USA, adding to the renaissance of straw bale building. They advocated both the loadbearing Nebraska technique and the use of straw bales as infill panels in timber constructions (Welsch 1970; Doolittle 1973; McElderry 1979; Strang 1983). Since 1993, there is the quarterly magazine *The Last Straw – The Journal of Straw Bale Construction (2.9)*. The sudden boom of straw bale building in the USA caused various states to enact specific building

2.10

2.11

2.12

regulations *(see chapter 20).* The first official directives in the USA were the "New Mexico Straw Bale Construction Guidelines" of 1991. In the 1990s, extensive research was conducted throughout the USA to establish reliable performance data on thermal insulation, loadbearing capacity, wind and earthquake resistance as well as behaviour in fire (King 2006). In the 1980s, the first workshops for the experimental construction of buildings had been carried out, first in the USA, later also in Canada and England. The first international conference on straw bale building was held in 1993 and led to the foundation of the National Straw Bale Research Advisory Network. Meanwhile, many more international networks for the proliferation of straw bale building were created, for instance the German association of straw builders, Fachverband Strohballenbau (FASBA), founded in 2002. In many countries, including the USA, Canada, Australia, England, Germany and Austria, there are professional contractors specialising in straw bale buildings.

The development in Europe and elsewhere

The first international conference on ecovillages, *Ecovillages and Sustainable Communities for the 21st Century,* was held in 1995 in Findhorn, Scotland, and became a point of departure for contemporary straw bale buildings in Europe. David Eisenberg held a workshop on straw bale construction at the conference, and in 1995 and 1997, further straw bale workshops were conducted by Martin Oehlmann and Harald Wedig in Germany, which resulted in a number of small test buildings *(2.10).* In 1998, a first straw bale conference took place in Plougonven in Brittany, France, which saw 50 participants. In Germany, the first straw bale building with a building permission was erected in Windeck-Werfen in 1999, designed by Ruth and Matthias

2.10 Test building, Recklinghausen, Germany, 1997 (Design: Martin Oehlmann, Harald Wedig)

2.11 Germany's first straw bale building with a building permission, Windeck-Werfen, Germany, 1999 (Design: Ruth and Matthias Bönisch)

2.12 Studio building Guhreitzen, Germany, 2000 (Design: Dirk Scharmer)

2.13 Farm building Wargoldhausen, Germany, 2001 (Design: Eva und Albert Warmuth)

2.14 Residential building, ecovillage Sieben Linden, Wendland, Germany, 2001 (Design: Björn Meenen, Martin Stempel)

2.15 Three-storey apartment building "Strohpolis", Sieben Linden, Germany, 2007 (Design: Dirk Scharmer)

2.16 Non-loadbearing straw bale vault, holiday residence, Bad Schussenried, Germany, 2007 (Design: Gernot Minke)

2.13

2.14

2.15

2.16

Bönisch (2.11). The first straw bale building with loadbearing walls was constructed in 2000 at the University of Kassel under the supervision of Gernot Minke and Dittmar Hecken (p. 80). Further projects were to follow in Germany, for instance the studio building in Guhreitzen, planned and built by Dirk Scharmer and erected with jumbo bales (2.12), or a two-storey farm building in Bavaria (2.13). In the ecovillage Sieben Linden in the German Wendland area, a residential building was erected by the users themselves without the aid of power tools (2.14). In 2002, the German association of straw builders was founded in Sieben Linden. Three years later, farmer and contractor Peter Weber built, near Trier, the first loadbearing building with jumbo bales that received a building permit (8.4, p. 44). In 2004, Gernot Minke with Friedemann Mahlke designed a non-loadbearing straw bale dome to be used as a rehearsal space in Forstmehren, Germany (9.1, p. 47). Also

in the village of Sieben Linden, a three-storey apartment building was designed and built by Dirk Scharmer (2.15). In 2007, Gernot Minke developed a non-loadbearing straw bale vault for a holiday residence in Bad Schussenried (2.16). In 2007, STROH unlimited in Buckow near Berlin was founded, Germany's first straw bale construction company. In 2009, Benjamin Krick designed an office building in Rai-Breitenbach (Breuberg) that used loadbearing, vertical jumbo bales (2.19). And in 2013, the first loadbearing straw bale vault that received a building permit was designed by Gernot Minke and Tobias Weyhe and built in Buchberg-Wangelin, Germany (p. 138). So far, approx. 900–1500 straw bale buildings have been built in Germany.

In Austria, considerable efforts were undertaken to establish straw as insulation material, supported by the programme "Haus der Zukunft" (House of the Future) by the Ministry for Traffic, Innovation and Technol-

2.17

2.18

2.19

2.20

2.17 Nordic Folkecenter for Renewable Energy, Hurup Thy, Denmark, 1998

2.18 Winery and storage building, Lethbridge, Australia, 1999 (Design: Huff 'n' Puff Constructions)

2.19 Office building Rai-Breitenbach, city of Breuberg, Germany, 2009 (Design: Benjamin Krick)

2.20 Five-storey apartment building, Amsterdam, the Netherlands, 2007 (Design: René Dalmeijer)

ogy and by GrAT (Gruppe für angepasste Technologien), led by Robert Wimmer *(see, e.g. the projects in Böheimkirchen and Tattendorf, p. 128 and p. 134)*. About 140 straw bale buildings have been realised in Austria. In Switzerland, Atelier Werner Schmidt has built a number of straw bale buildings, including a three-storey load-bearing structure in Italy *(p. 122)*.

Both in Ireland and the UK, the all-women building firm Amazon Nails has been active since 1989. In 2003, founder Barbara Jones built her first project in Ireland, the iconic Spiral House *(p. 10)*. Some 700 straw bale projects have been built in Ireland, some 2000 straw bale houses in the UK.

Probably the earliest straw bale house in Scandinavia was built in 1956 in Norway *(2.7)*. In the past 20 years, Rolf Jacobsen, part of Gaia Arkitekter, designed many straw bale buildings in this country. In Denmark, the Nordic Folkecenter for Renewable Energy in Hurup Thy was a pilot project supported by the Danish Ministry for Construction that was completed in 1998 *(2.17)*. It has since had an enormous influence on the development of straw bale construction in Scandinavia.

In Slovakia, several straw bale projects have been realised, including the first loadbearing dome in 2010, designed by Gernot Minke *(p. 140)*. An example from the Netherlands is a five-storey timber frame construction with straw bale infill *(2.20)*. In France, even a seven-storey apartment building was erected in 2013 *(p. 108)*. According to a survey by FASBA (Fachverband Strohballenbau Deutschland e.V.), about 2500 straw bale buildings were realised in that country.

In Belarus a whole settlement for displaced families from Chernobyl was built which received the "World Sustainable Energy Award" in 2000. Supported by the government, some 200 straw bale buildings could be realised in that country (Wedig 1999). Finally, Australia has a very active straw bale building community with many interesting examples. One of the largest loadbearing straw bale buildings was erected in 1999 in Lethbridge *(2.18)*: it is a 250-m² winery building with storage and vending facilities; the 4.6-m-tall walls are made of 220 jumbo bales measuring 90 × 90 × 240 cm. The bales have a weight of about 225 kg and were erected with the help of a front-loader in three days.

3 Straw as a building material

General facts

The term straw denotes the dry stalks of threshed grain (wheat, rye, barley, oats, millet) or fibrous plants (flax, hemp, rice). Straw is a regenerative resource that develops out of photosynthesis using solar energy, water and minerals in the ground. It consists of cellulose, lignin and silica and possesses a waxy, water-repellent skin. Due to its high silica content, straw rots extremely slowly. In agriculture it is, therefore, frequently used for the de-compacting of soil, as ground cover in stables or as a fodder additive in winter. Only rarely is straw used as fuel or for the production of straw panels. Most suitable for the production of bales for building is wheat, spelt and rye straw – as opposed to barley and oats, which are less stable. For centuries, straw was used throughout Europe to thatch roofs (although it should be mentioned here that reed is more suitable since it is more durable). As an aggregate to the building material clay it has been used for millennia to increase thermal insulation and reduced the risk of crack formation during drying of the material (for further information, see Minke 2013, chapters 4, 9 and 10).

Straw bales

Type and quality of the straw mostly determine the qualities of the straw bale. For the production of bales to be used for construction long, unbroken stalks are preferable.

Mowing and threshing

The grain plant is harvested when it has reached a stage of overripeness, i.e. when the grains are hard and dry and the stalks yellow and brittle. A combine harvester *(3.1)* then cuts the stalk roughly 10 cm above the soil and feeds the stalks from the mower into the threshing unit. Depending on how the straw is guided through the threshing unit one can distinguish tangential and axial combine harvesters.
In a harvester with a tangential thresher mechanism, the grain moves through a thresher drum and thresher concave. Beater

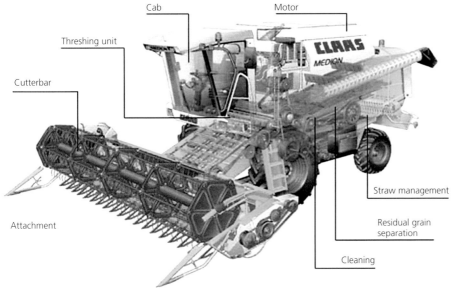

3.1

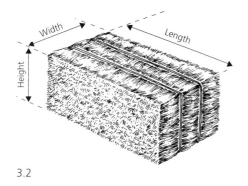

3.2

bars attached to the drum then beat the grains out of the ears. The gap between threshing drum and threshing concave is crucial for the harvest: the narrower it is the larger the amount of grain separated from the ears but the stalks are often damaged in the process (Büermann 1999). After passing the threshing unit, the crop is fed into a straw walker where the residual grain is separated from the straw. The grain then fills a grain tank while the straw falls to the ground behind the threshing unit and forms a linear mound of straw, the so-called windrow.

Very large, modern combine harvesters have an axial thresher mechanism around which the straw circulates a number of times. The beater bars push the grain out of the ears, which leaves the grain mostly intact but damages the straw so badly that it is mostly reduced to chaff. Harvesters with both axial and tangential units also exist; the axial unit then functions as the

straw walker. However, they also do great damage to the straw.

Since the use of undamaged straw stems results in bales of higher stability, it is advisable that the straw for bales is harvested by a combine with a tangential unit. This is of particular importance if the bales are used in a loadbearing capacity.

Baler	Bale dimensions [cm]		
	Height	Width	Length
Small bale press	31 (30)	41 (40)	30–120
	36	49 (48)	50–120
Square baler	50	80	70–240
	70	80	120–250
	70	120	90–300
	90	120	100–270
	100	120	100–300
	130	120	100–270

3.3

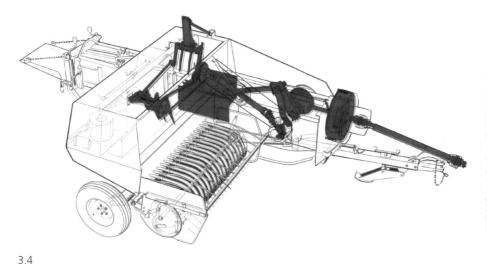

3.4

3.5

3.6

3.7

3.8

3.9

3.10

Straw baling

Small bale presses and square balers can be used to produce straw bales suitable for buildings. Bales created by round balers can be recycled and pressed into rectangular bales. Height and width of the bale are determined by the dimensions of the bale chamber and cannot be changed *(3.2)*. The bale length can be modified to some extent. Typical bale dimensions and formats are shown in figure *3.3*.

With small bale presses *(3.4–3.7)* a bale density of up to 120 kg/m³ can be reached (according to the manufacturer's specifications). The dimensions of the bale are typically 36 × 49 × 50 cm to 130 cm. These small bales are usually bound together by two (rather than three) strings. Small bale presses are in use at small farms and their sales figures are steadily going down. Many manufacturers of agricultural machines have ceased making them, in favour of square balers and round balers.
Big square balers have been the most recent development. They can reach a density of up to 220 kg/m³ and dimensions of 80 cm to 120 × 70 cm and 130 × 80 cm

to 300 cm. The bales are bound with four or six strings. They are common at large farms and agricultural companies. In the USA, three-string balers are often used which produce bales of 41 × 56 × 46 cm to 132 cm which are bound by three strings.

Straw bales for buildings

Straw bales designated for use in buildings should have a number of characteristics:

– Bound by plastic or wire
– Bale ends must not be rounded
– Straw stalks mostly undamaged (harvested with combine with tangential unit)
– Golden yellow colour (not grey or black)
– No mouldy odour
– Dense bale structure, strings should be tight
– Relative humidity within bale lower than 75 % (equivalent to a mass-related humidity below 15 %)
– Minimum density of 90 kg/m³ and 110 kg/m³, if the bales are used for a loadbearing construction

3.1 Parts of a combine harvester, here Claas Medion

3.2 Height, width and length of the straw bale

3.3 Typical straw bale dimensions

3.4–3.7 Small bale press, here Welger AP 56

3.8 Loose bale

3.9 Dense bale

3.10 Square baler, here Claas 3400

During the harvesting process, straw stalks must remain largely undamaged. Straw must then not be exposed to rain. If straw becomes moist and then dry again, it becomes brittle. Constant moisture can result in mould and decay within the bale and damage by micro-organisms.

While sisal tying strings are ecologically preferable, tests have shown that the durability of natural fibres is insufficient. If the bale edges are sharp, accurate and without rounded parts (3.9), the construction process is more efficient as no time is lost for aligning the bales and filling the gaps between them. Bales of low density and inaccurate edges (3.8) require more labour if used in construction. They need to be trimmed (bale ends have to be even), stalks that stick out have to be cut before plastering and densification might also be necessary.

When pressing straw bales for construction purposes, the following rules apply:

– Windrows should have even dimensions
– Cranks at baling chamber for adjustment of bale density must be firmly tightened
– A baling chamber can be tightened further by lateral inliners which increase bale density by approx. 4 % per centimeter
– The pickup unit should always be completely full
– The baler should be driven at a high and constant speed over a large and even windrow

Straw bales that are used for construction must meet the following criteria:

1. Visual inspection: A bale is not suitable if
   a) the binding strings consist of natural fibres
   b) the bale shows discolouration
   c) the edges are rounded
   d) the bale includes weeds as weeds are less stable and will decay faster when damp.

2. Haptic and olfactoric inspection:
   A bale is not suitable if it is moist to the touch or if it smells mouldy.

3. Load test: One should be able to stand comfortably on a flat-lying bale without sinking in. The binding strings should not loosen up.

4. Moisture test: The sensor of a hygrometer is (4.10) introduced into the centre of a bale. The relative humidity in the bale must not exceed 75 %.

5. Density: For non-loadbearing applications, the minimum density should be 90 kg/m³. If bales are used in a loadbearing construction, the density must be at least 110 kg/m³.

Straw bales have to be stored in a dry environment, that is, they must not touch moist ground directly and must be protected from rain. On site they are best stored on pallets.

4   The building physics of straw

Horizontal straw fibres

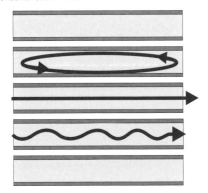

Vertical straw fibres

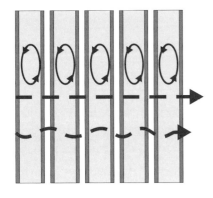

Convection

Thermic conduction

Radiation

4.1

Heat conductivity

In principle, there are three options for heat transmission: radiation, convection and thermic conduction. While thermal radiation transmits energy by means of electromagnetic waves and can penetrate both translucent materials or a void, both convection and thermic conduction need a medium to work. Thermic conduction is the transport of heat through a material. Generally speaking, one can say that dense materials conduct heat easier than materials of low density; therefore, low-weight materials do not transmit heat easily and are thus suitable to provide thermal insulation. Heat transmission through convection occurs when thermal energy is transmitted to a passing (moving) medium such as air or water.

In order to calculate the insulation performance of a building component, both the thermal conductivity of a material and the thickness of the component have to be known. Thermal conductivity is abbreviated with Lambda (λ) and is measured in $W/(m \cdot K)$. A thermal conductivity value of $\lambda = 2\,W/(m \cdot K)$ means that 2 Watt thermal energy is transmitted through a 1-m-thick wall over a wall surface of $1\,m^2$, given a temperature difference of $1\,°C$ between the interior and the exterior of the wall. With straw bales, heat conductivity varies with the orientation of the stalks. If the heat transmission happens parallel to the straw fibres, the heat conduction capacity is

higher as if the heat is transmitted vertically in relation to the fibres (4.1).

According to the general building supervision approval for straw bales, the following heat conductivity values can be assumed:

Heat transmission parallel to stalk orientation: $\lambda = 0.080\,W/(m \cdot K)$

Heat transmission vertical to stalk orientation: $\lambda = 0.052\,W/(m \cdot K)$

When compared to plastic or mineral fibre insulation materials which have values of $\lambda = 0.024$ to $0.045\,W/(m \cdot K)$, these are relatively high heat transfer coefficients. However, when compared to softwood ($\lambda = 0.13\,W/(m \cdot K)$), this is a favourable value.

Heat transmission resistance

The heat transition coefficient (U-value) of a wall indicates the amount of thermal energy transmitted at a temperature delta of 1 Kelvin through a wall surface of $1\,m^2$. The lower the U-value, the less energy is transferred and thus the lower the costs for heating. Therefore, it is important that all exterior components of a building have a relatively low U-value.

The U-value of a component consisting of n material layers can be determined as follows:

$$U = \frac{1}{R_{Si} + \dfrac{d_1}{\lambda_1} + \dots + \dfrac{d_n}{\lambda_n} + R_{Se}}$$

with:

U Heat transition coefficient [W/(m²·K)]

R_{si} Interior thermal boundary resistance [m²·K/W]

d_1 Density of the 1st material layer [m]

λ_1 Thermal conductivity of the 1st material layer [W/(m·K)]

d_n Density of the nth material layer [m]

λ_n Thermal conductivity of the nth material layer [W/(m·K)]

R_{se} Exterior thermal boundary resistance [m²·K/W]

Figure *4.2* shows the U-values of straw bale wall constructions with the following build-up (from interior to exterior): 4 cm earth render, straw bale, 2 cm earth render, ventilated boarding. The depth of the straw layer is determined by the available bale sizes. The table compares the values with those achieved with conventional insulation materials and timber of the same thickness.

Heat storage

Generally speaking, one can say that a material of high density also has a high heat storage capacity but transmits heat more easily as well. The lighter a material, the better its insulation capacity and the lower its heat storage capacity. However, these physical correlations are rules of thumb only and reality is more complex. Organic materials can store almost twice as much thermal energy as mineral materials of the same density, and water can even store four times as much energy. Each material has a specific heat storage capacity c. This storage capacity is a material constant which is usually expressed in kJ/(kgK). The absolute storage capacity C, given as kJ/K of an object with a specific volume, can be calculated as follows:

$$C = c \cdot \rho \cdot V$$

with:

c Material-specific heat storage capacity [kJ/(kg·K)]

ρ Density of a material (kg/m³)

V Volume mass (m³)

In order to measure the usable thermal energy Q stored in a volume and describe it in kJ, the heat storage capacity of the volume C has to be multiplied with the temperature difference between the volume and its surrounding:

$$Q = C \cdot \Delta T \text{ [kJ]}$$

with:

C Heat storage capacity of the volume (kJ/K)

ΔT Temperature difference between volume and surrounding (K)

For the conversion of Q in (Wh) the following applies:

3.6 kJ = 1 Wh or 1 kJ = 1/3.6 Wh

Figure *4.3* shows that the heat storage capacity of straw is quite good when compared to other insulation materials but rather low when compared to solid building materials. For instance, a timber frame wall or a roof construction with a U-value of 0.15 W/(m²·K) where straw is used for insulation will achieve a heat storage capacity ten times higher as the same construction with a mineral fibre insulation; moreover, the thermal comfort will be considerably higher.

When compared to a massive wall construction, a lightweight construction insulated with straw will of course have a significantly lower heat storage capacity (assuming the same U-value). In order to improve the heat storage capacity of straw bale walls it is useful to apply earth plaster to the wall interior with a high rate of sand and fine gravel. With a specific volume weight of 1900 to 2100 kg/m³ and a thickness of 3 to 6 cm, the plaster layer contributes to shielding the interior from temperature fluctuations. The heat storage capacity and the user comfort inside are further improved if the interior walls consist of 11.5-cm-thick adobe, brick or sand lime stone masonry. Moreover, abobe and to some extent also earth plaster has a regulating effect on room humidity.

Thermal bridges

Thermal bridges denote patches on walls or roofs that have a significantly lower thermal resistance than adjacent areas. This means that at these patches, heat transition from the inside out is substantially higher than at areas with high thermal resistance. Consequently, they increase heat losses of the building and can even cause moisture or mould problems due to the formation of condensate. This can lead to serious problems in the areas in question if there is no sufficient vapour proofing: moisture-affected areas will provide even poorer thermal insulation and, in the case of straw, may assist growth of moulds, spores and bacteria.

Risk areas for thermal bridges at straw bale walls are – for instance – unfilled gaps between bales or junctions with door and window frames. But even the wooden post-and-beam structure can form a thermal bridge since the thermal conductivity of wood is two to three times higher than that of straw bales. It is therefore advisable to reduce or avoid timber components that penetrate the straw bale wall in its entire depth.

Moisture protection

Building components and in particular exterior walls have to be protected against moisture in order to avoid damage to the building. Excessive humidity can be caused by driving rain, by moisture rising up from the soil or by condensation of water in the interior.

Horizontal seals against rising humidity

Building regulations in Germany stipulate that walls must be protected from rising humidity from the building ground by horizontal seals – regardless of whether it is a solid or lightweight construction. The sealing can consist of bituminous, synthetic or metal sheeting.

Thickness of straw layer (m)	U-value of wall [W/(m²·K)]
Heat flow vertical	
0.31	0.16
0.36	0.14
0.50	0.10
0.70	0.07
0.90	0.06
1.00	0.05
1.30	0.04
Heat flow parallel	
0.41	0.19
0.49	0.16
0.80	0.10
1.20	0.07

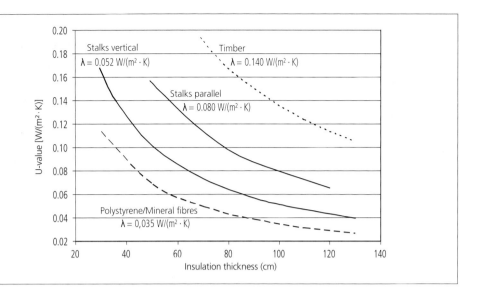

4.2

Specific heat storage capacity C [kJ/(kg·K)]	
Metals, e.g. aluminium	0.90
steel	0.45
Mineral materials	approx. 1.00
Organic materials	approx. 2.00
Water	4.20
Storage capacity C [Wh/(m³·K)]	
Steel	988
Aluminium	675
Reinforced concrete	694
Cellular concrete	125
Timber	278
Straw (110 kg/m³)	56
Cellulose fibres (55 kg/m³)	29
EPS (18 kg/m³)	10
Mineral fibres (27 kg/m³)	6
Water	1167
C [Wh/(m²·K)] at U= 0.15 W/(m²·K)	
Straw (110 kg/m³)	19.3
Cellulose fibres (55 kg/m³)	7.7
EPS (18 kg/m³)	2.3
Mineral fibres (27 kg/m³)	1.6

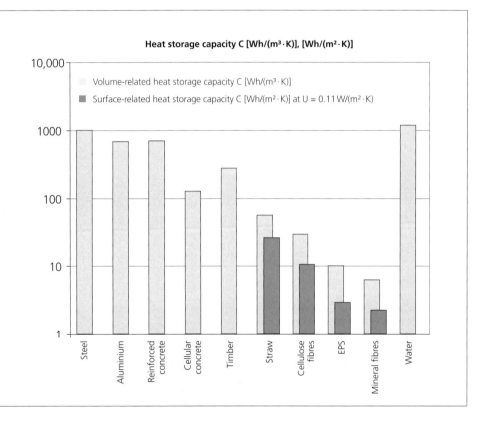

4.3

4.1 The heat conduction capacity in relation to the stalk orientation

4.2 U-value of straw bale walls in relation to thickness and stalk orientation

4.3 Heat storage capacities of various building materials

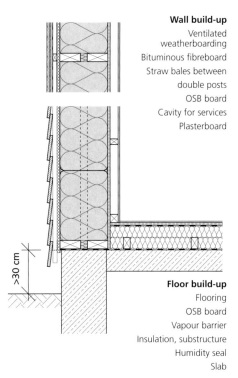

Wall build-up
Ventilated
weatherboarding
Bituminous fibreboard
Straw bales between
double posts
OSB board
Cavity for services
Plasterboard

Floor build-up
Flooring
OSB board
Vapour barrier
Insulation, substructure
Humidity seal
Slab

>30 cm

4.4

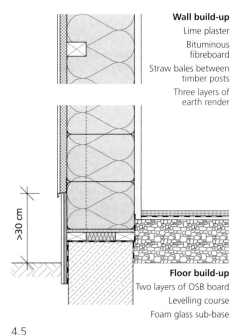

Wall build-up
Lime plaster
Bituminous
fibreboard
Straw bales between
timber posts
Three layers of
earth render

Floor build-up
Two layers of OSB board
Levelling course
Foam glass sub-base

>30 cm

4.5

Splash water protection

All walls must have a splash boarding at the base up to a height of at least 30 cm above grade or a flat roof. Ideally, the first layer of straw bales should start above this height *(4.4)* or a splash protection consisting of splash boarding or special plaster has to be provided *(4.5)*. The risk of splash water can be reduced significantly by a gravel or crushed stone bed or a dense and low vegetation at the perimeter *(4.7)*. Hard surfaces, e.g. paving, in front of the wall will have the reverse effect *(4.6)*.

Weather protection

Like any other wall, a straw bale wall needs to be protected from rain, hail and wind. This can be achieved with a weatherproof plaster free of cracks or – more preferable – by ventilated weatherboarding *(see chapter 12)*.

Hygroscopic behaviour of straw

Hygroscopy is the capacity of a material of attracting, holding and emitting water molecules from the surrounding air. In humid conditions, the strong hydrophilic behaviour of straw fibres leads to a high level of moisture absorption. Since this can affect their structural properties, the underlying physical processes of hygroscopy need to be understood.

Relative humidity (RH or ϕ) is defined as the ratio between the current water vapour in the air (given in g of water per m³) and the maximum moisture in the air, the saturation humidity (also g/m³). Relative humidity is expressed as a percentage. If the relative humidity is 1, respectively 100 %, the air is saturated and cannot absorb any more water. The higher the air temperature, the more humidity can be absorbed. If the air temperature decreases, the relative humidity will rise and may reach a maximum of 1 (100 %). If the air becomes colder yet, condensation will occur, i.e. water in its liquid form will be emitted. If a material is exposed to a constant relative humidity and temperature over an extended period

of time, a material-specific water content will be reached which is called equilibrium moisture content υ (g/g). According to DIN EN ISO 12571 (2000) it is defined as follows:

$$u = \frac{m - m_0}{m_0}$$

The mass of the humid volume is described by m while m_o describes the mass of a completely dry volume. The process of intake of water by a material from the air is called absorption, the process of release of water is called desorption. Sorption is used as the generic term for both processes. The equilibrium moisture content of a material at a constant temperature and different air humidity levels is represented in sorption isotherms. If the relative humidity of the air surrounding a volume is known (which can be measured fairly easily), this isotherm will describe the humidity of the volume if a temperature equilibrium between volume and air exists. Figure *4.8* shows the sorption curves of wheat, barley, rye and spelt straw at 23 °C (Krick 2008).

Vapour diffusion and the formation of condensate

Due to the vapour pressure gradient – which, in heated rooms in our climate, runs from the interior to the exterior – the water vapour in the air will find a way through the separating building element. This process follows the physical laws of pressure balance and is called diffusion. The resistance of a material to the diffusion of water vapour in the air is called vapour diffusion coefficient μ and it is also determined by the thickness of the material. This μ-value depends on the density and pore structure of the respective material.

The product of vapour diffusion coefficient m and the thickness s of the building element equals the resistance to water vapour diffusion and is given as the diffusion-equivalent air layer thickness s_d [m]. Air has a vapour diffusion coefficient of 1; this means, for example, that a building element with $s_d = 10$ m has the same

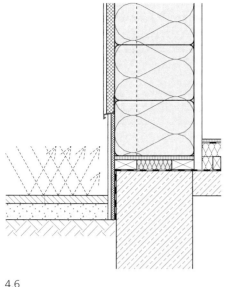

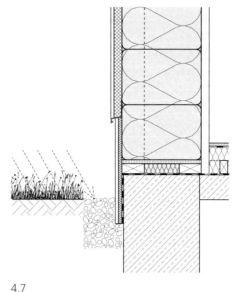

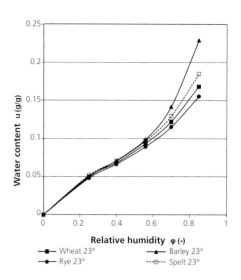

4.6

4.7

4.8

4.4 Bales above splash water zone (top horizontal section, below vertical section)

4.5 Splash water zone with protected bales (top horizontal section, below vertical section)

4.6 Splashing on hard surfaces

4.7 Reduction of splashing by vegetation or gravel

4.8 Sorption isotherms for wheat, barley, rye and spelt straw at 23°C

resistance to water vapour diffusion as a 10-m-thick air layer.

As a rule of thumb, resistance to water vapour diffusion of the individual layers of a wall should decrease from the inside out so that the diffusion is not blocked by a more dense layer. If, however, a layer of high diffusion density is on the outside, which is the case with straw bale walls that are rendered with earth on the inside and with cement on the outside, vapour diffusion will be obstructed by the more vapour-resistant cement plaster; this may cause formation of condensate on the inside of the cement render. This is due to the low μ-value of earth render of 6 to 8 and – in contrast – the high μ-value of cement render of 20 to 30 (12.3).

Even if the interior render were two to three times thicker than the exterior render, the resistance to water vapour diffusion of the exterior render would still remain substantially higher. The problem could be solved with an exterior lime render with a μ-value of 10. Alternatively, the vapour diffusion resistance of the interior earth render would have to be increased by a moisture-proof, vapour-resistant coat of paint. The μ-value of straw bales is approx. 2 and thus relatively low (AbZ 2006). Generally speaking, absolute humidity within the straw bales must remain below 15 %. A short-term higher humidity does not lead to rotting, though.

In spaces with a humidity of more than 70 % – for example bathrooms – it is advisable to increase the resistance to water vapour diffusion of the interior render, for example by additives like linseed-oil varnish or resistant coats of paint like latex or linseed-oil varnish (see chapter 12).

A vapour barrier course is usually not required for a vapour-permeable wall with exterior lime plaster or ventilated weatherboarding. With regard to the early straw bale buildings in Nebraska (with its dry climate), which were plastered with cement and had no vapour barrier, there are no reports on damages as a result of condensate. While it can be assumed with certainty that condensate will form inside the wall, the quantities are small, will evaporate and thus not lead to mould.

Measurement of moisture content

Due to the inhomogeneous structure of straw, it is difficult to determine its moisture content. An exact determination is possible only by comparing the specific weight of the bales before and after drying. However, a rather exact determination is possible by employing sorption isotherms. Such isotherms were established in (Krick 2008) and they are shown in 4.9.

In order to establish the moisture content of a straw bale with this method, a probe is introduced into the bale and the relative air humidity and the temperature in the bale is measured. A hygrometer as used in the agrarian sector or a simple household hygrometer with an external sensor can be used. In this case the sensor with an extended cable is attached to a spear and then introduced into the bale (4.10). The result will be charted on the x-axis and the moisture content can then be determined – based on the sorption isotherm – on the y-axis (4.9). The chart comprises temperatures of 15 and 25°C. For other temperatures, the values can be interpolated in a linear fashion.

Development conditions for mould

As it is the case with all organic building materials, mould can grow on straw bales and can lead to decay, if favourable conditions such as a high air humidity and warm temperatures exist. Moulds can decompose organic materials, lead to damage to the building and emit toxic substances. They can cause mycosis, mycotoxicosis and mycogenic allergies (Sedlbauer 2001). However, not all types of mould are dangerous. They thrive in a temperature

range between 0 and 50°C. The speed of biomass build-up depends on the temperature and is at its maximum between 20 and 30°C, depending on the mould type. Mostly minor variations in temperature will determine whether spores can germinate. Once they have germinated and formed an initial mycelium, mould is rather resistant against unfavourable temperatures. If adverse temperatures persist, the mould fungus will slow down or stop its growth altogether. When the temperature becomes more conducive again, it will resume its activities. The main criterion for the growth of mould is the available moisture. In practice one can assume that no mould development will occur if the relative air humidity is below 70%.

In respect to their suitability for mould fungi, materials can be divided in four substrate groups 0–III (Sedlbauer 2001). Substrate group 0, optimal breeding ground, comprises all biological complete media. Substrate group I, biologically usable substrates, are building products of easily composable raw materials such as wallpapers or gypsum plasterboard. Substrate group III, inert substrates, consists of metals, foils, glass and tiles.

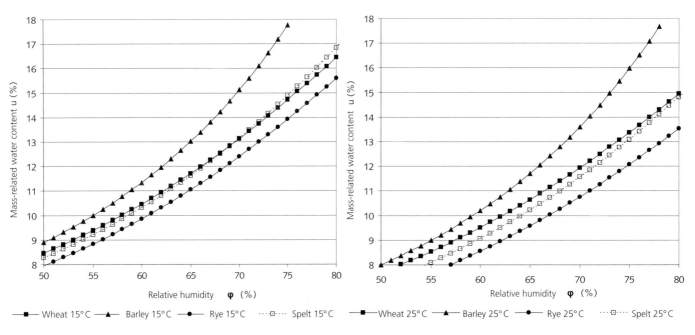

4.9

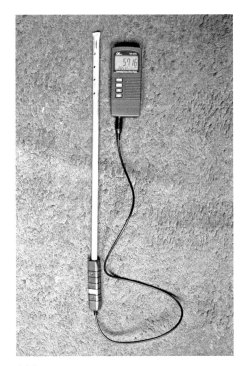

4.10

Substrate	Maximum moisture content for mould prevention
Wheat	0.13 g/g
Barley	0.15 g/g
Rye	0.12 g/g
Spelt	0.13 g/g

4.11

4.9 Sorption isotherms of wheat, barley, rye and spelt straw at a temperature of 15° C (left) and 25° C (right)

4.10 Hygrometer for determination of humidity and temperature within the bale

4.11 Maximum moisture content that will warrant absence of mould, for various types of straw classified as substrate group I

4.12 Suitable and partially suitable constructions in respect to mould susceptibility

Construction diagram	Layer thickness (cm)	Build-up	Suitability (annual mould growth in mm)
		Weatherboarding	Suitable
	3	Battens with air layer	
	2.2	Wood fibreboard (or earth render 3 cm)	
	36	Straw bales	
	1.5	Gypsum plasterboard or OSB board or OSB board with 2-cm clay building board	
Build-up as above but with a 85-cm straw bale layer			Limited (6 mm)
		Weatherboarding	Limited (41 mm)
	3	Battens with air layer	
	3	Three-layer earth render	
	36	Straw bales	
	3	Three-layer earth render	
Build-up as above but with an interior earth render layer as vapour barrier (μ = 30)			Limited (43 mm)
Build-up as above but with a softwood fibreboard instead of the interior render			Limited (58 mm)
		Weatherboarding	Limited (16 mm)
	3	Battens with air layer	
	2	Lime-cement plaster	
	24	Masonry	
	2	Lime-cement plaster	
	36	Straw bales	
		Vapour barrier (s_d = 2 m)	
	1.3	Wood boarding	
	3	Three-layer earth render on reed mat	
		Roof tiles, battens, counter battens	Suitable
	2.2	Softwood fibreboard	
	36	Straw bales	
	1.5	OSB panel	
		Vegetation, substrate layer, drainage layer, root barrier membrane, non-woven, roof membrane	Suitable
	2.8	Tongue-and-groove boarding	
	4	Air layer	
	2.2	Softwood fibreboard	
	36	Straw bales	
		Vapour barrier (s_d = 2 m)	
	2.2	Boarding	
	2	Earth render on reed mat	
As before but without air layer and softwood fibreboard			Limited (31 mm)
	2	Earth render or 2.2-cm softwood fibreboard	Suitable
	36	Straw bales	
		Optional: vapour barrier (s_d = 2 m)	
	2.2	Boarding	
	2	Clay building board or earth render on reed mat	

4.12

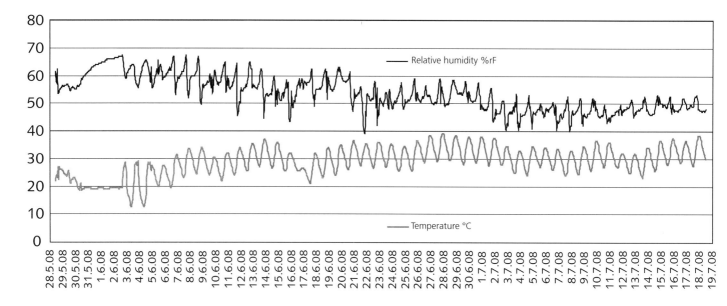

4.13

Initially, straw was classified in substrate group I; according to research undertaken by Fraunhofer Institute for Building Physics in Holzkirchen, it was downgraded into group 0 (FASBA 2008). Investigations of built examples, however, indicate that straw in practice can be classified between group I and II (FASBA 2008). Assuming a substrate group of I, one can derive from the sorption isotherms the mass-related moisture content that will warrant absence of mould (4.11).

Another factor is time. The shorter a substrate is exposed to a climate conducive to mould growth, the less likely the development of mould.

In order to predict the growth of mould, complex transient observations of temperature, moisture, nutrient medium and time are needed. Prediction programmes such as WUFI Bio, which take mathematical models of mould spores into account, can deliver such prognoses. The result is a mould growth in mm. This indicates the amount of activity.

The Centre for Environmentally Conscious Building (ZUB) at the University of Kassel conducted extensive hygrothermic simulations of various wall constructions (FASBA 2008). According to this research, only those wall types can be fully recommended where the straw bales have an exterior insulation layer and an additional weatherproof boarding.

Constructions without an insulation layer may be suitable if additional weatherproofing is provided. Alternatively, a construction where the insulation layer is substituted by a 3-cm earth render is also a good option. These recommendations apply to small bales. Constructions with jumbo bales can be used for some applications when they have an insulation layer and weatherproofing. Without weatherproofing, driving rain can soak the render and lead to mould growth. Without insulation layer, the exterior of the bales is colder than the interior and condensate can form, which in turn may lead to mould growth. Suitable to a certain degree is the use of an interior straw bale insulation for an existing wall with an exterior boarding and insulation layer if an additional vapour barrier (s_d = 2 m) on the interior is provided. With pitched roof constructions, only the version with an interior OSB board, exterior insulation layer, counter battens, battens and roof tiles was classified as completely non-hazardous. For flat roof constructions, a ventilated turf roof was recommended and a turf roof without air layer was recommended to a degree. Completely unobjectionable are straw bales as insulation of the top floor slab under a pitched roof.

Figure 4.12 gives an overview of various wall and roof constructions in respect to their susceptibility towards mould (FASBA 2008). A construction is classified as of limited suitability if the annual mould growth is below 150 mm. The straw vaults that were built in 2007 in Tamera in Portugal (p. 136) have a bituminous membrane directly on top of the earth-rendered straw vaults, covered with a green roof. There is no vapour barrier on the interior. In this type of build-up the interior insulation is not protected from condensate so that moisture damage is a potential problem. If massive formation of condensate on the interior bituminous membrane occurs, due to the temperature difference between the interior and the exterior, and if the condensate cannot diffuse into the interior quickly enough, damages can be the result. Given Portugal's warm climate and the insulating green roof, this is not a major problem. In order to monitor the humidity at the roof membrane, a temperature and humidity sensor was installed that recorded data in June and July 2008 (4.13).

The diagram shows that relative humidity (albeit during the summer) was not critical as the medium exterior temperature was consistently higher than the medium temperature within the building. These data show that condensate that perhaps accu-

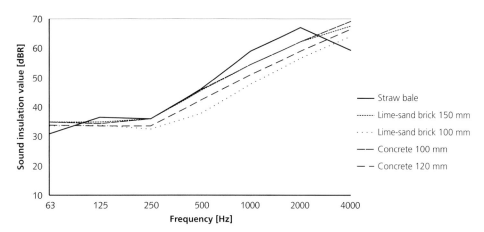

4.14

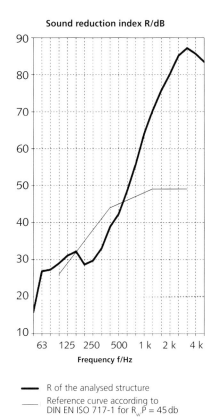

Sound reduction index R/dB

R of the analysed structure

Reference curve according to
DIN EN ISO 717-1 for R_wP = 45 db

4.15

mulated in the winter could be diffused. It is likely that the wall build-up is suitable also in the long run. However, this may not be the case for other climates.

Sound protection

Air-borne sound insulation mainly depends on the weight (mass) of a building element: the greater the weight of a wall, the better is the air-borne sound insulation it will provide. Sound insulation of straw bales with double-sided plastering is higher than that of single-layered elements of the same weight. This fact can be attributed to a certain vibration of straw bales, and bales will also absorb sound to a certain degree.

In Australia, tests were conducted on 45-cm-thick walls of a sound studio: at a noise level of 114 to 117 dB inside the building, 62 to 71 dB were measured outside within a frequency spectrum of 500 to 10,000 Hz. This amounts to a noise level difference of 43 to 55 dB (John Glassford in GrAT 2001).

Figure 4.14 shows the sound reduction index of a 45-cm-thick straw bale wall with an apparent density of 120 to 130 kg/m³ and untreated 2.5- to 3.5-cm earth render as established at Technical University Eindhoven, the Netherlands. In the diagram, it is compared to the index of solid concrete and lime-sand brick walls.

The Institute for Acoustics and Building Physics in Oberursel, Germany, determined the sound reduction index for a post-and-beam wall with 36-cm straw bale infill and with a 1-cm-thick plaster on both sides at 43 dB (FASBA 2008). Another wall with a 1-cm-thick earth render on one side and a 2-cm-thick earth render on the other side had a value of 44 dB. Figure 4.15 shows that the sound reduction index rating is low with low frequencies, then rises with increasing frequency, reaches its lowest point at 200 Hz and then goes beyond 80 dB at a frequency beyond 500 Hz (FASBA 2008).

4.13 Temperature and humidity data in the Living vaults in Tamera, Portugal

4.14 Sound reduction index of various materials

4.15 Sound reduction index of a post-and-beam wall with straw bale inflll and 1-cm-thick earth render on both sides

4.16

4.17

Fire protection

Building materials are classified with regard to their fire resistance over a defined length of time as follows: F30, F60, F90, F120. In steps of 30 minutes, these classifications highlight the capability of the respective materials to maintain their essential functions such as structural integrity and the enclosure of space.

Loose stalks of straw are easily inflammable, similar to a single sheet of paper. However, straw pressed into a bale is much harder to ignite as is the case with a phone book consisting of many individual pages of paper tightly bound.

Authorised research in Germany established an F30 rating for a post-and-beam wall construction with straw bale infill and an (at least) 1-cm-thick earth render on both sides. For loadbearing straw bale walls with 3- to 5-cm-thick earth plaster on each side the rating was F30 as well (FASBA 2008). In 2014, a timber frame construction with straw bales and 8-mm lime plaster was successfully tested and achieved a fire resistance of 90 minutes (FASBA 2014). In Austria, a non-loadbearing straw bale wall with interior earth render and exterior lime render was tested and likewise assigned an F90 fire rating. Related tests in the USA (SHB AGRA test) even established a fire resistance of 120 minutes (Steen et al. 1994).

The high fire resistance of a plastered straw bale wall can be attributed to the high fire rating of the render itself as well as the high compression of the bales not leaving enough oxygen for the combustion of straw. Even if the plaster contains cracks, a charred exterior straw layer will be formed preventing the entrance of further oxygen. This result was established in a test installation at the Research Laboratory for Experimental Building at the University of Kassel under high temperature conditions of 1000 °C. Even after 90 minutes, no fire broke out and only a charring of the bales occurred in those areas where the plaster had cracked.

Without plaster, i.e. while under construction, exposed straw bale walls may pose an increased fire hazard due to protruding straw stubbles. Therefore, they should receive a first plaster layer right after completion of the wall structure. For best results, a pump should be used to spray and immerse all stalks evenly (4.16, 4.17).

4.16 Application of first plaster layer
4.17 Straw stalks enclosed by earth render

5   CO$_2$ content and primary energy content of straw bales

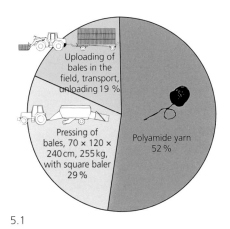

Uploading of bales in the field, transport, unloading 19 %

Pressing of bales, 70 × 120 × 240 cm, 255 kg, with square baler 29 %

Polyamide yarn 52 %

5.1

5.1 Primary energy content of large bale production and proportion of process steps

Principles

For the production of every building material energy is needed. The less intensely processed a building material is, the less energy was used for its manufacturing. Therefore natural building materials such as clay, natural stones or timber contain significantly less production energy than industrially processed building materials like metals, plastics or concrete. The energy that was required for the production of a building material is its primary energy content (PE).

The primary energy content comprises all preparatory and manufacturing processes until the product is ready for delivery. Only energy from non-renewable sources is considered (Kohler/Klingele, eds., 1995). Hence the primary energy content describes the amount of non-renewable energy that is required to manufacture a (building) product. Solar energy stored as carbon for instance in timber or straw is also not taken into account and neither is the energy used for the transport of the building materials to the construction site and for installation. Like any other plant, wheat (which in turn becomes straw) grows with the help of photosynthesis and extracts CO$_2$ (carbon dioxide, a gaseous molecule with one atom of carbon and two atoms of oxygen) from the air. The carbon is used for the structure of the plant, while the oxygen is released into the air. After dying the plant rots. In this process the carbon reacts with the

oxygen from the air. This oxidising creates exactly the same amount of CO$_2$ as the plant stored in its growth phase. Therefore the process is CO$_2$ neutral. If the plant is burned, the process is the same but with significantly accelerated oxidation.

By using straw as insulation material, it is removed from this process because the carbon remains bound in the straw bale and neither by combustion nor by rotting released into the atmosphere. The straw bale house thus becomes a carbon store. Straw has a carbon content of approx. 42 %. Thus, a tonne of straw stores 420 kg of carbon. The atmosphere is relieved of approx. 1.5 kg of CO$_2$ per kg of straw for the duration of its use in the building. The CO$_2$ emissions avoided in this way is credited to the building's energy balance. However, if the straw is burned after use in the building (or composted), it has to be evaluated like a fossil fuel.

Primary energy content of straw bales

The primary energy content (PE) of large bales has been determined at 50 kWh/t and of small bales at 63 kWh/t (Krick 2008). The baling itself, the primary energy content of the bale yarn, loading and transport processes as well as the type of machines used and their proportionate manufacturing costs were considered as well for these values. When large quantities are needed, large bales have a lower primary energy

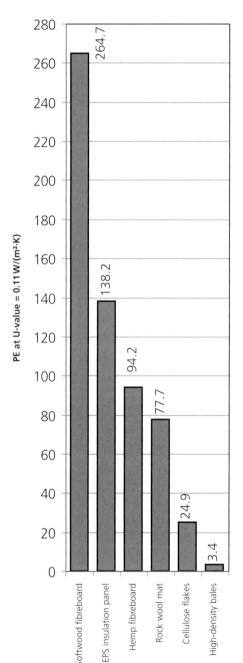

content than small bales, despite the loading processes by machines. This is due to the higher efficiency of modern square balers. Figure 5.1 shows the proportion of the individual process steps in the manufacture of large bales within the overall primary energy content. The high proportion of bale yarn is striking. This is not because the bale yarn has a very high primary energy content, the reason is rather that the other process steps cause extremely low expenses (Krick 2008).

Primary energy content of various building materials and constructions

Straw bales are primarily used for thermal insulation. Figure 5.2 shows the PE of different insulation materials based on a U-value of 0.11 W/(m² · K) which is usually sufficient to reach passive house standard in a single-family home. Clearly, the straw bale insulation has the lowest primary energy requirement. The assumption that insulation materials from renewable raw materials would in all cases have a lower primary energy content than those from fossil-based or mineral-derived materials is wrong. The by far highest primary energy content is attributed to softwood fibreboard (manufactured in the usual wet process). The rock wool mat has a lower PE than hemp insulation. This may be surprising because hemp is harvested in the field, just like straw. However, hemp is cultivated specifically for the production of insulation while straw is a waste product. Therefore the energy needed for growing the grain is

not taken into account. If the processes of cereal cultivation were considered, the PE for straw would be in the realm of cellulose flakes also depicted in 5.2.

However, wall constructions comprise not only the insulation. Figure 5.3 compares the primary energy content of conventional build-ups with straw bale constructions. The point of departure is a sand-lime brick wall with a thermal insulation composite system of extruded polystyrene (EPS), rendered with resin on the outside and with a lime cement plaster on the inside (construction type 1 in 5.3).

The primary energy content is embodied in roughly equal parts in the loadbearing construction (i.e. the sand-lime brick) and the insulation, as well as to a lesser degree in "other", in this case the plaster layers. If the EPS is replaced by a wood fibreboard (construction type 2), the energy requirement for the insulation is greatly increased. The use of straw bales in place of the softwood fibreboard clearly gives evidence of the extremely low PE of the bales (construction type 3). For further reduction of the PE, the loadbearing sand-lime brick layer is replaced by CLT, thereby reducing primary energy consumption for this component and also for the "other" elements, because no interior plaster is necessary as the timber remains exposed.

If the massive CLT panel is replaced by timber I-joists and the exterior plaster by wood boarding, the use of straw bales will result in a slight reduction of the PE. Through the use of rock wool or cellulose no further savings can be achieved. The primary

5.2

energy demand of the wood/straw construction is only slightly lower, because the OSB used on the inside and the softwood fibreboards attached on the outside have a higher volume-related PE than the CLT. The reason is that more energy is required for the insulation, since the I-joists have to be insulated up to the flanges with softwood fibreboards.

Further savings can be attained, if earth render is used instead of the OSB panels on the inside and of the softwood fibreboards on the outside (construction type 8). If type 8 is built without I-joists, a loadbearing straw wall structure is the result (construction type 9). Type 9 performs best here and with 10 % of primary energy of the first construction type.

The following should be noted:

1. An undisturbed wall section was considered here without any edge details. If these are included, the PE is higher.
2. Regarding the formation of mould, type 7 has been classified by the Centre for Environmentally Conscious Building (ZUB) at the University of Kassel as hygrothermally suitable, while types 8 and 9 have only limited suitability in this respect. Types 3 and 4 are not recommended since they have a considerable risk of mould growth, according to the calculations of WUFI Bio. In summary it can be stated that the primary energy requirement of exterior walls can be reduced significantly through the use of straw bales. The classifications of construction types 5-8 are transferable to roof structures.

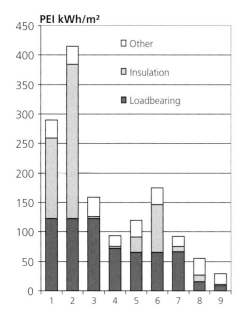

1. Thermal insulation composite system: lime-sand brick/EPS
2. Thermal insulation composite system: lime-sand brick/wood fibre
3. Thermal insulation composite system: lime-sand brick/straw
4. Thermal insulation composite system: CLT/straw
5. Lightweight timber, insulated by cellulose
6. Lightweight timber, insulated by rock wool
7. Lightweight timber, insulated by straw/OSB
8. Lightweight timber, insulated by straw/earth
9. Loadbearing straw

5.3

5.2 Primary energy content of various insulation materials at a U-value of 0.11 W/(m² · K)

5.3 Primary energy content of various building materials and wall constructions with a U-value of 0.11 W/(m² · K)

6   Structural design principles

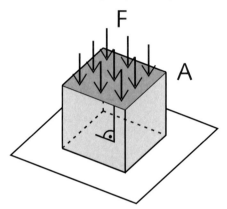

The stress s results from the force F [kN] acting on the surface A [m²].

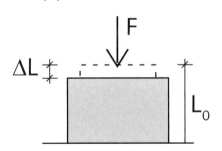

The deformation is calculated from the reduction of ΔL [m] relative to the original element height L [m]

6.1

Slenderness

Slenderness is defined as the ratio of wall height to wall thickness and is a measure of a wall's resistance to buckling. The greater the slenderness ratio, the less stable the wall will be. For loadbearing structures, the Californian Straw Bale Building Code specifies a maximum ratio of wall height to wall width of 6:1 (King 2006). With small bales laid flat, an unbraced wall height of 0.48 m × 6 = 2.88 m (minus compaction due to [pre-]compression) can be achieved, which is sufficient for residential buildings and many other applications. With small bales laid on edge, a maximum unbraced wall height of 0.36 m × 6 = 2.16 m is possible. To achieve normal room heights in this case, the bale wall needs to be placed on an additional stem wall. More slender walls are possible if additional bracing is provided.

Compression

When a load is applied to a building element, it produces a deformation, typically a displacement resulting from compression. A measure of resistance to deformation is the modulus of elasticity (also known as Young's modulus, E [kN/m²]), which is the ratio of the stress σ [kN/m²] caused by a load to the resulting proportional deformation ε [m] (6.1). The higher the modulus of elasticity of the building material, the stiffer the wall (Krick 2008).

The modulus of elasticity of straw bales depends primarily on the bale density and the orientation of the straw fibres. The denser the bale, the higher the modulus of elasticity. Bales laid flat have a lower modulus of elasticity (where straw bale construction is concerned) than on-edge bales (6.2). When bales are laid flat, the stalks lie horizontally on top of each other and squash under load. When bales are laid on edge, the stalks stand upright next to each other like hollow straws, which makes them more resistant to compression but also more susceptible to buckling (Krick 2008).
Straw bale walls have a higher modulus of elasticity than individual straw bales and larger bales have a higher modulus of elasticity than small bales (6.3).
Plastering straw bales increases the modulus of elasticity significantly. A key factor here is how the force is applied to the wall. If the load is introduced directly into the plaster skin, the modulus of elasticity is higher than if the load is applied to the bales.
The fact that wall elements have a higher modulus of elasticity than individual bales can be explained by the inability of bales within a wall to extend in length under load as they are held in place by their neighbours. Figure 6.3 shows the moduli of elasticity of straw bales and wall elements made of straw bales.
Figures 6.3–6.5 show that:
– Bales laid on edge have a higher stiffness than bales laid flat.

– Large bales have a higher stiffness than small bales.
– Restrained or prestressed bales and walls are more rigid than regular bales or bale walls, since lateral restraint hinders the lateral expansion of the bales. This is likewise the case for bales within a wall.
– Walls made of small bales are more rigid than individual small bales. This is because the bales in the wall impede the transverse extension of neighbouring bales. The effect is stronger than in the case of small bales that were restrained laterally.
– Plastered small bales and plastered bale walls have a much greater rigidity than those that have not been plastered.

The fact that a plaster coat contributes significantly to the stiffness and thus the loadbearing capacity of a wall can be seen clearly by comparing the curves in figures 6.4 and 6.5: while an unplastered wall of small bales laid on edge exhibits approx. 9% compression at an applied load of 40 kN/m², the compression of the corresponding wall when plastered and indirectly loaded is only approx. 0.5%. All data in figures 6.4–6.9 according to Krick (2008), except for large bales, laid flat (6.4, Schmidt 2003) and the wall of small bales (6.5, Zhang/Fairie 2002). In the case of direct loading, where the load is applied directly to the plaster, the degree of compression is even lower, as seen in the corresponding tests with single bales: an indirectly loaded, plastered small bale laid flat exhibits approx. 3.7% compression at a load of 30 kN/m², but only approx. 0.3% when directly loaded. The influence of partial load application on the loadbearing behaviour is discussed on p. 39.
Tests with small bales showed that straw bales loaded with 40 kN/m² regained approx. 70–80% of their initial height within the first few minutes after removal of the load. As such, a 20–30% degree of compression remained. Straw bales therefore exhibit semi-elastic deformation (Krick 2008). This results in a higher stiffness when loaded again. It can therefore make sense to use pre-compressed bales for loadbearing walls.

Creep

When initially loaded, a building material responds with spontaneous deformation, typically compression. Sustained load over a longer period can cause further deformation within the material, which is known as creep.
Figure 6.6 shows the total compression of a small bale over a period of 30 days after application of a load. The total compression is made up of the initial compression, which occurs immediately when the load

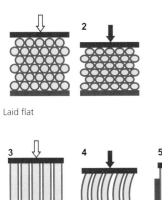

Laid flat

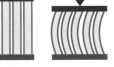

Laid on edge

6.2

Material (wheat straw)	Density [kg/m³]	Modulus of elasticity E [kN/m²]
Small bales, laid flat Small bales, laid flat (prestressed)	112[1] 107[1]	258[1] 312[2]
Small bales, laid on edge Small bales, laid on edge (prestressed)	109[1] 99[1]	256[1] 375[2]
Small bales, turned on end	98[1]	169[2]
Medium bales, laid flat	124	750[3]
Medium bales, laid on edge	110[1]	821[2]
Small bales, plastered, laid flat, direct load	106[1]	5486[2]
Small bales, plastered, laid flat, indirect load	112[1]	911[2]
Small bales, plastered, laid on edge, direct load	93[1]	7418[2]
Small bales, plastered, laid on edge, indirect load	84[1]	1240[2]
Wall element, small bales, laid flat	95[1]	417[2]
Wall element, small bales, laid on edge	98[1]	661[2]
Wall element, plastered small bales laid on edge	–	29,000–89,000[4]
Wall element, plastered jumbo bales laid flat	–	4900[3]
For comparison (Läpple 2006) Concrete (for example) Iron Wood (spruce) Rigid PVC (for example)		$30 \cdot 10^6$ $210 \cdot 10^6$ $10 \cdot 10^6$ $3,5 \cdot 10^6$

The values from different sources are only comparable to a limited extent.
[1] Dry density;
[2] (Krick 2008), +/- 20%, values apply up to a tension of 40 kN/m²;
[3] (Danielewicz/Reinschmidt 2007) at 40–60 kN/m²;
[4] (Grandsaert 1999).

6.1 Modulus of elasticity, stress, compression
6.2 Elasto-mechanical behaviour of bales laid flat and on edge
6.3 Modulus of elasticity of straw bales and straw bale wall elements (sources: see last row of the table)

6.3

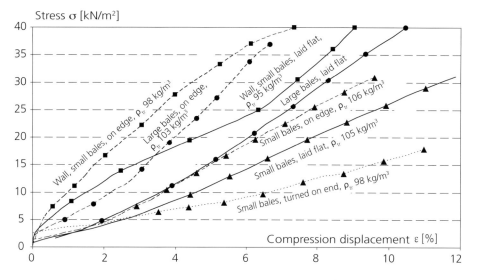

Stress σ [kN/m²]

Wall, small bales, on edge, ρ_tr = 98 kg/m³
Large bales, on edge, ρ_tr = 103 kg/m³
Wall, small bales, laid flat, ρ_tr = 95 kg/m³
Large bales, laid flat
Small bales, on edge, ρ_tr = 106 kg/m³
Small bales, laid flat, ρ_tr = 105 kg/m³
Small bales, turned on end, ρ_tr = 98 kg/m³

Compression displacement ε [%]

6.4

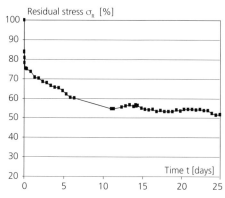

Residual stress σ_R [%]

Time t [days]

6.7

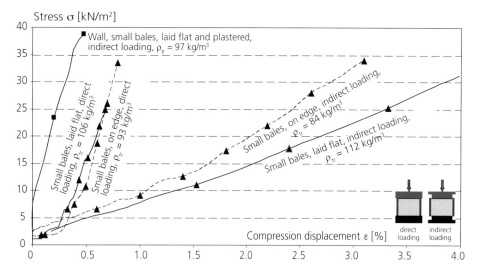

Stress σ [kN/m²]

Wall, small bales, laid flat and plastered, indirect loading, ρ_tr = 97 kg/m³
Small bales, laid flat, direct loading, ρ_tr = 106 kg/m³
Small bales, on edge, direct loading, ρ_tr = 93 kg/m³
Small bales, on edge, indirect loading, ρ_tr = 84 kg/m³
Small bales, laid flat, indirect loading, ρ_tr = 112 kg/m³

Compression displacement ε [%]

direct loading   indirect loading

6.5

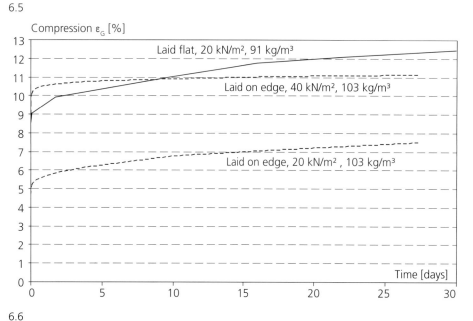

Compression ε_G [%]

Laid flat, 20 kN/m², 91 kg/m³
Laid on edge, 40 kN/m², 103 kg/m³
Laid on edge, 20 kN/m², 103 kg/m³

Time [days]

6.6

6.4 Stress-strain diagram of restrained (clamped) wall elements made of on-edge and flat small bales, flat and on-edge and upright small bales and flat and on-edge medium bales. The densities given are dry densities. All individual bales were restrained laterally during the tests. All single bale characteristics are average values of at least three tests (except for medium bales laid flat). The curves are comparable with each other due to the same or similar test set-up, except for medium bales laid flat.

6.5 Stress-strain diagram of a restrained (clamped) earth-plastered wall element made of flat small bales and restrained plastered walls made of small bales laid flat and on edge with direct and indirect load application. The densities given are dry densities. All single bale characteristics are average values of at least two tests. The curves of the single bales are comparable due to the same test set-up.

6.6 Creep behaviour of small bales laid flat and on edge at a tension of 40 or 20 kN/m²

6.7 Stress relaxation of walls made of unplastered small bales, laid flat, with a dry density of 95 kg/m³ after an initial load of 40 kN/m²

6.8 Behaviour of partially loaded bales laid flat and on edge

6.9 Wall deformation in horizontal load testing (the deformation of plastered walls is given in mm, that of unplastered walls in cm).

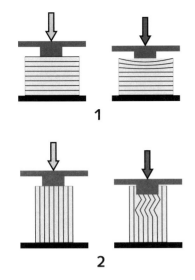

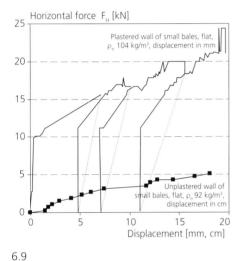

6.8

Horizontal force F_H [kN]

Plastered wall of small bales, flat, ρ_{tr} 104 kg/m³, displacement in mm

Unplastered wall of small bales, flat, ρ_{tr} 92 kg/m³, displacement in cm

Displacement [mm, cm]

6.9

is applied, and the creep deformation. The tests were conducted on prestressed individual bales. As has been demonstrated, walls exhibit lower initial deformation and probably also lower creep deformation. According to Smith, no further creep is observed in unplastered walls of laid-flat bales after approx. 15 weeks, while creep behaviour continues in walls made of on-edge bales for approx. 44 weeks (Smith 2003). In the case of large bales (often called jumbo bales), creep behaviour declines more rapidly due to their higher density.

Relaxation

When, after applying a force to a test specimen, the level of displacement (deformation) is kept constant over time, the level of stress within the test specimen starts to reduce, a characteristic known as relaxation. The walls of a loadbearing straw bale building are compressed when the roof is added, as well as when roof loads increase, for example due to snow loads. To mitigate against this, loadbearing straw bale walls are prestressed, i.e. the settlement resulting from higher loads is anticipated. The amount of pre-compression must be higher than the maximum occurring load to take account of relaxation. Tests have shown that the stress relaxation of loadbearing walls made of flat small bales to which an initial load of 40 kN/m² was applied, amounts to approx. 50 % after 25 days (Krick 2008) (6.7).
For 85-cm-thick walls made of jumbo bales, Danielewicz/Reinschmidt determined a stress relaxation of approx. 46 % after 30 days at an initial load of 120 kN/m². After six weeks, virtually no further stress relaxation was observed.
To take account of stress relaxation in loadbearing walls, the amount of pre-compression must be correspondingly higher. It is, however, hard to apply this level of compressive stress on the construction site. In addition, special measuring equipment is required to determine stress levels. It is therefore advisable to start from a degree of

compression that can be easily measured. In practice, it makes sense to first let the full roof load act on the walls until no more wall settlement can be measured. Once the wall has settled, only the maximum snow load then needs to be taken into account in pre-compression.
Another possibility is to apply pre-compression gradually, making it possible to successively apply a significantly lower level of compressive stress. This method has been tried and tested in practice but has not yet been scientifically investigated.
It should be noted that the above information applies to small bales. Large bales are already more intensively compressed and exhibit better compression and possibly therefore also better creep and relaxation behaviour.
In other parts of the world, it is widely recognised that plaster in combination with straw bales sustains a substantial part of the load. This has been clearly proven in load testing but is at present not permitted for use in structural calculations in Germany.

Partial load application

In loadbearing straw bale constructions, a ring beam crowns the top of the bale wall. This can incur significant costs, especially with large bale constructions, which can be reduced if the ring beam does not have to span the entire width of the wall. In Krick (2008) and Danielewicz/Reinschmidt (2007) the effects of partial load application on stress-strain behaviour and stress relaxation were investigated.
For small bales laid flat, Krick determined that the modulus of elasticity sank by approx. 20 % when the load was applied to 42 % (= 20 cm) of the bale width. The impact of partial load application on stress relaxation was not significant. Danielewicz/Reinschmidt arrived at similar results for jumbo bales laid flat when the load was applied to 43 % (= 51 cm) of the bale width. For small bales laid on edge, Krick determined that the modulus of elasticity sank by approx. 60 % when the load was applied to

56 % (= 20 cm) of the bale width. The level of relaxation was about 8 % higher than the values determined for fully loaded bales. The results show that the modulus of elasticity of partially loaded straw bales is lower than that of fully loaded bales, irrespective of the orientation of the straw fibres. The effect is much more pronounced when the bales are laid on edge rather than flat. It would seem that a partially applied load is better distributed when the bales lie flat (see 1 in 6.8) than when they are on edge (see 2 in 6.8). The reduction of the modulus of elasticity of the wall only affects the uppermost bale layer of laid-flat bale walls. For walls made with on-edge bales, it is recommended to load the full width of the wall.

Deformation of walls under horizontal load

Horizontal loads occur as a result of wind pressure and must be dissipated into the foundations by means of bracing. In masonry construction, the wall itself is sufficiently resistant to horizontal loads. In lightweight timber construction, diagonal boarding, panel sheathing, or diagonal cross braces, corner braces or wind bracing steel ribbons provide the necessary stiffening.
Plastered straw bale walls can absorb horizontal loads, such as those resulting from wind, better than unplastered straw bale walls. In Germany, however, it is not permissible to apply the effects of plaster in structural load calculations, and additional bracing measures must therefore be provid-ed for straw bale constructions, just as they are for lightweight timber construction. The California Straw Bale Building Code (King 2006) allows plaster to be considered as a statically effective component, depending on the type of plaster and reinforcement. For example, a horizontal load of 1.5 kN/m is permitted for non-reinforced clay plasters, and a load of 2.6 kN/m for plastic-reinforced clay plasters. For a lime-cement plaster with screed mat reinforcement, loads of up to 6.6 kN/m are permissible (see figure 6.10).
The results of tests carried out by (Krick 2008) on 2-m-high walls made of laid-flat small bales are shown in figure 6.9. For an unplastered wall, prestressed with 40 kN/m², a horizontal load of 5 kN applied at the top of the wall resulted in a lateral deformation of 180 mm, whereas the lateral deformation of a plastered wall under the same conditions but with a higher horizontal load of 15 kN was only 6 mm.

Seismic performance

The seismic performance of straw bale constructions is excellent due to their high elasticity. At the University of Nevada in Reno, USA, a low-cost prototype of the "Pakistan Straw Bale and Appropriate Building" (www.paksbab.org) was subjected to a biaxial vibration test. The 3.5 × 3.5 m building with loadbearing straw bale walls withstood an extreme acceleration of 0.82 g.

Plaster	Plaster reinforcement	Shear stress [kN/m]
Earth	none	1.5
	Hemp mesh, 8-cm mesh size	1.8
	Polypropylene mesh, 5-cm mesh size	2.6
Lime	Wire mesh	3.0
	Screed mat (2-mm wire gauge, 5-cm mesh size)	3.6
Lime-cement	Wire mesh	5.8
	Screed mat (2-mm wire gauge, 5-cm mesh size)	6.6
Cement	Wire mesh	5.8
	Screed mat (2-mm wire gauge, 5-cm mesh size)	8.8

6.10 Permissible shear stress according to the California Building Code.

6.10

7   Passive houses with straw bale insulation

A passive house is a building that has an annual heating energy requirement of no more than 15 kWh/(m²·a), corresponding to an annual consumption of approx. 1.5 l of oil per square metre of living space. This low heating energy requirement is achieved through excellent thermal insulation and high-quality windows with triple-pane insulating glazing, good airtightness of the construction with no thermal bridges and the use of a ventilation system with waste heat recovery.

At such low heating energy levels, the remaining heat still required can usually be introduced via the (hygienically necessary) fresh air supply of the ventilation system, obviating the need for a separate heating system. The cost savings can instead be invested in the quality of the building's thermal envelope.

Passive houses are on average 5–8 % more expensive to build than conventional buildings. However, the additional costs are amortised by the energy savings during operation over the course of the building's service life.

For residential buildings in the passive house standard, the heat transfer coefficient of external walls should be no more than UAW = 0.15 W/(m²·K). For detached single-family houses, however, this value is usually not sufficient to achieve the critical value for the annual heating energy demand of 15 kWh/(m²·a). In such cases, U-values of less than 0.11 W/(m²·K) are recommended (see, for example, Feist 2001).

These low U-values can be achieved with on-edge or on-end bales of straw with an insulation thickness of approx. 50 cm or more and a thermal conductivity value of $\lambda = 0.052$ W/(m·K). The use of small bales is possible with supplementary external insulation (which is stipulated in any case by the previously mentioned general building regulations). Figure 7.1 shows three examples of straw bale wall constructions suitable for passive houses. Using narrow window frames and especially high-performance glazing, it is, however, also possible to achieve passive house standard without supplementary external insulation of the straw bales.

Thermal bridges must be avoided as far as possible in passive houses. Special attention must therefore be paid to the position and design of ring beams, thresholds, posts and floor-to-wall junctions.

A high degree of airtightness is a prerequisite for the proper functioning of ventilation systems with waste heat recovery. The airtight layer must be arranged on the inside of the insulation for reasons of building physics. If the airtight layer is provided by a render coat of earth plaster, it must be adequately reinforced to ensure no cracks can occur that extend the entire depth of the plaster coat. Other possibilities include the use of building foils or papers as well as panel materials with bonded or sealed joints. Transitions between material must be planned and executed with particular care.

Small bales, on edge with external insulation 51 cm
– Earth plaster, 5 cm
– Straw bale, on edge, 36 cm
– Softwood fibreboard, 10 cm
– Earth plaster, 2 cm
– Sheathing

├── 51 cm ┤

Large bales, on edge 57 cm
– Earth plaster, 5 cm
– Straw bale, on edge, 50 cm
– Earth plaster, 2 cm
– Sheathing

├── 57 cm ──┤

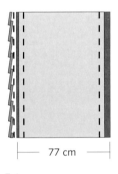

Large bales, laid flat 77 cm
– Earth plaster, 5 cm
– Straw bale, laid flat, 70 cm*
– Earth plaster, 2 cm
– Sheathing
* nearest standard bale size: 80 cm

├── 77 cm ──┤

7.1

Ventilation systems with waste heat recovery are a central component of the passive house concept. In air-to-air heat exchangers, the cold fresh air supply flows past the warm exhaust air without mixing, absorbing some of its heat in the process. The air flows are driven by fans. Assuming the system is correctly designed and uses high-quality components, the operation of the fans requires only a fraction of the energy saved through heat recovery. Filters protect the ventilation system against clogging and are replaced annually. They also retain dust and pollen, which is beneficial for allergy sufferers.

As several of the case studies in this book show, the low embodied energy of straw bale constructions and the low heating energy requirement of the passive house concept complement each other optimally in the creation of sustainable and liveable buildings. For more information on the topic of passive houses see www.passivehouse.com.

7.1 Wall constructions with straw bale insulation suitable for passive house standard

8   Wall construction systems

Definitions and construction principles

There are two substantially different construction systems:
First, there is the loadbearing straw bale wall where the roof loads are transmitted into the foundation directly via the straw bales (8.1). In the literature, the loadbearing straw system is frequently called "Nebraska technique" due to its invention in Nebraska in the late 19th century.
The second type is the non-loadbearing straw bale wall system, usually consisting of a loadbearing timber frame construction or a post-and-beam construction with straw infill panels or face straw bales (8.2). The frame structure transmits the roof loads and stabilises the wall; here, the straw bales have no structural purpose and exclusively serve for thermal insulation. Timber panel constructions or nail-laminated timber constructions are options as well, with the straw bales positioned in front of the loadbearing timber wall. This type of system is also used in energy rehabilitation where straw bale insulation is applied to existing wall constructions. In principle, straw bale infill can also be used for concrete or steel skeleton structures. However, the risk of thermal bridges and potential damage needs to be considered carefully. In 1982, the Canadian Louis Gagné developed a loadbearing wall system (mortared bale matrix system), also known as "Gagné technique": the bales are laid like bricks on cement mortar forming cross-joints. The resulting pattern of vertical and horizontal joints performs – fully or partially – the loadbearing task (8.3). This system, however, entails the formation of thermal bridges and is consequently not suitable for colder climates – which is why this book will not deal with it in great detail (Steen, et al. 1994). There are also hybrid systems with the straw bales partially performing loadbearing tasks and partially only functioning as infill panels. Oftentimes, supposedly loadbearing straw bale systems are – strictly speaking – hybrid constructions. In the Spiral House in Ireland (p. 10), the chimney stack absorbs a part of the roof and ceiling loads, and in the loadbearing straw houses in Trier (8.4) and Disentis (8.5), the glazed south façades contributes to the loadbearing task. It is important to consider the differences in settlement behaviour of the various loadbearing systems in order to avoid damages later.

Loadbearing straw bale walls

Walls made out of stacked straw bales, which transmit the roof loads directly into the foundations, are so compelling because of their structural simplicity and the short construction time and low cost, respectively. Therefore, they proliferated quickly throughout the USA after the invention of straw bale presses in the late 19th century (see pp. 13–15). Although no one will dispute time and cost savings even today, the

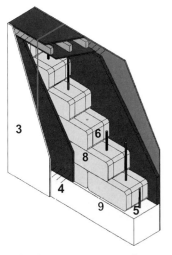

1 Clay plaster
2 Clay fine plaster
3 Lime plaster
4 Plaster reinforcement
5 Anchor bolt
6 Nail
7 Tightening strap
8 Straw bale
9 Ring beam

8.1

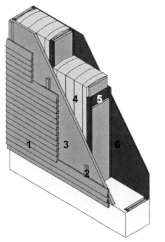

1 Weatherboarding
2 Battens
3 Soft fibreboard
4 Straw bale
5 I-joist
6 OSB panel

8.2

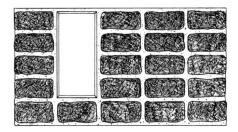

8.3

8.4

8.5

heavy dependence on the weather during construction is an issue. Loadbearing straw bale walls impose restrictions on the size of the building and planning permissions remain a problem as well, in particular in Germany. So far, loadbearing straw bale buildings have been officially approved on an individual basis. This contrasts with the situation in Switzerland, Austria and Italy where planning permissions have already been granted for buildings of that type of up to three storeys (p. 122). By and large, design of loadbearing straw bale buildings is restricted to single-storey buildings. This is due to the fact that the ratio of wall height to wall thickness should not exceed 6:1 and that the recommended maximum load of 20 kN/m². By using large bales and hybrid systems, these restrictions can be addressed to some extent. This will be discussed at greater detail in chapter 11, p. 52, 53.

An essential requirement for loadbearing walls is that bales are relatively well compressed and that walls are prestressed. To achieve this, a ring beam on top is required, which is then connected to the foundation with tension ties. The prestress of the tension ties inside the wall should ideally be slightly higher than the roof loads so the bales will not receive further compression. The prestress can be created with rods

threaded through the centre of the bales or interior and exterior tensioned straps (8.6). If tensioned rods are used they have to be threaded in through the bales, which is time-consuming and requires the rods to be segmented. Therefore, this technique is hardly ever used these days. There is also the risk of condensation occurring around the rods which can lead to mould growth. A simpler method involves tensioned straps, although here well-balanced prestressing can be difficult and the straps might hamper finishing works. Figure 8.10 shows various types of prestressing systems (Krick 2008). Many tests have shown that the plaster layers contribute to stabilising the walls and that they absorb part of the loads. However, this effect cannot be calculated and can therefore not be used for obtaining a building permit.

Non-loadbearing straw bale walls

In non-loadbearing straw bale walls the straw bales have no structural function. The loadbearing construction usually consists of timber components (8.7). Straw bales have an insulating purpose and often create the wall facing in combination with plaster. They can be used as infill between the loadbearing components of a frame or

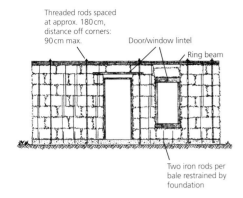

Threaded rods spaced at approx. 180 cm, distance off corners: 90 cm max.

Door/window lintel

Ring beam

Two iron rods per bale restrained by foundation

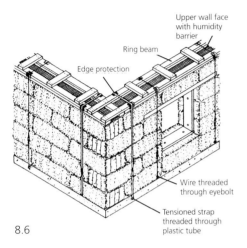

Upper wall face with humidity barrier

Ring beam

Edge protection

Wire threaded through eyebolt

Tensioned strap threaded through plastic tube

8.6

skeleton construction or they form a continuous layer on the outside or the inside of the post-and-beam construction. Figure *11.8* shows five options for positioning the timber posts. The straw bales must always be connected to the loadbearing structure to make sure the bales or the straw layer cannot become dislodged. If frame systems are clad with panels or a diagonal boarding these elements can provide structural stiffness to the walls and brace them against horizontal loads such as wind.

With a skeleton system struts or diagonal steel ribbons can provide bracing as well. Rendered straw bales also add stiffness to the construction but, depending on the country, it may not be possible to take this into account fort he structural analysis.

Straw bale shell in a new building

A version of a non-loadbearing straw bale wall is a massive wall insulated with a straw bale layer *(8.8. 8.9)*. The wall can be built from CLT or glulam and absorbs both vertical and horizontal loads. The straw bales are attached to the wall by baler twine and eyelets and their function is only to provide insulation. The wall can then either be plastered or clad with boarding.

An example for this kind of system is the S-House in Austria *(p. 128)*.

Straw bale shell in an existing building

Another kind of use for straw bales is the supplementary facing of existing walls with straw bales acting as an exterior thermal insulation layer.

For existing buildings with a poor thermal performance, the application of an exterior straw bale shell can be an expensive and energy-efficient solution, if a time-saving assembly system is used or if the work happens in a low cost labour environment. The straw bales can either form a continuous layer that is firmly attached to the existing wall *(8.9)* or an exterior post-and-beam structure holds the bales in place. This has the additional advantage that a rear-ventilated boarding can be attached to the post-and-beam construction. However, a disadvantage is that fire can easily spread across the facade. It is recommended that earth render is applied to the exterior, making sure that no straw stubbles protrude from the surface.

The insulation layer increases the thickness of the wall significantly. The additional weight of the insulation needs to be absorbed, either by additional foundations or by attaching the straw bale shell to the existing exterior wall. The layer also creates deep window reveals and a potential need for longer roof overhangs.

8.1 Loadbearing straw bale wall system

8.2 Non-loadbearing straw bale wall system

8.3 Gagné system

8.4 Residence in Trier, Germany, 2005 (Design: Peter Weber)

8.5 Residence in Disentis, Switzerland, 2002 (Design: Atelier Werner Schmidt)

8.6 Prestressing of loadbearing straw bale walls

8.7 Post-and-beam construction with vertical straw bale infill (left elevation, right axonometric)

8.7

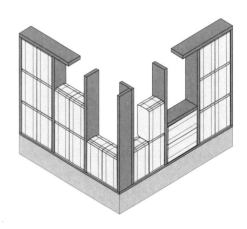

1 Dead load

2 Forklift or telescopic handler

3 Interior rods

4 Pneumatic lifting jack

5 Tensioning straps

8.10

8.8

8.9

Summary and comparison of the individual systems

– Loadbearing straw bale wall structures are by far more economical than non-loadbearing structures.

– They can be erected much faster and require fewer planning efforts and less trade skills for construction.

– They are the prototype of straw bale building.

The problem of this building method in Germany and some other countries is the lack of authorisation by local planning authorities, although it has been tried and tested for more than 100 years in the USA and has meanwhile been used for buildings with planning permission in Denmark, France, Great Britain, Holland, Ireland, Austria and Switzerland. No evidence against its stability, fire resistance or durability could be produced. The types of loadbearing structures that have been built in the USA and Canada with vertical and horizontal mortar joints are not suitable for North and Central European climates due to the formation of thermal bridges. As

far as the non-loadbearing systems – with straw bales used as facing insulation layer or infill panels – are concerned, they boast the advantage of low cost and excellent thermal insulation – these systems, on the other hand, face disadvantages because of the need for wider foundations, deeper embrasures and greater roof overhangs. Whether such a straw bale house is more economical than a conventionally insulated building cannot be answered with a clear yes or no; the answer will depend on planning, site organisation and many other factors. The unambiguous advantages are the environmental benefits: straw is a material that does not produce any carbon dioxide or other environmentally toxic emissions during production but – on the contrary – absorbs carbon dioxide from the air during photosynthesis. Another advantage is the fact that straw bales are inexpensive and can be used for do-it-yourself construction, which usually leads to cost savings. Furthermore, straw bale insulated buildings can achieve passive house standard (see chapter 7).

8.8, 8.9 Straw bale shell positioned in front of a massive wall. Residence in Lienzingen, Germany.

8.10 Various prestressing systems

9 Vaults and domes

9.1

9.2

9.3

Building barrel vaults and domes from bales of straw can be particularly economical and aesthetically pleasing. If the vaults start directly above the foundation, they simultaneously form the wall and roof of the building.

In 2003, a straw bale dome was erected over a structure of laminated wooden arches in Forstmehren in the Westerwald region of Germany (9.1).

In 2007, a straw bale vault structure was used for a holiday residence in Bad Schussenried. The arches made of nailed boards at 75-cm spacings and horizontal battens at 30-cm intervals formed the supporting framework for the straw bales stacked on top. The vault takes the form of a structurally optimal inverted catenary curve. The bales were post-tensioned with straps and coated with earth plaster on both sides. Lapped weatherboarding made of larch over a vapour permeable membrane serves as the external skin (9.2, 9.3).

Loadbearing straw bale vaults are even more economical. To make these, the straw bales need to be cut conically so that they can be laid in an arch without mortar or open joints (9.7). To this end, a special cutting apparatus (9.4) was developed at the Research Laboratory for Experimental Building (FEB) at the University of Kassel. The three housing units shown in figure 9.7 were built using this technique in Portugal in 2007 (see p. 136).

In 2009, an improved cutting apparatus was developed at the FEB to make it possible to simultaneously conically cut two sides of the straw bale with extreme precision (9.5). Such a device is needed for constructing a loadbearing dome, as planned by Gernot Minke for a project in 2010 (9.9). This building consists of a central loadbearing straw bale dome 6 m in diameter and eight loadbearing barrel vaults that serve as seating niches. The central dome stands on an octagonal ring beam and is erected without formwork using a rotating guide. All vaults are pretensioned with webbing and then covered with a green roof using local vegetation. The new cutting apparatus in figure 9.5 can also be used to construct shallow barrel-vaulted ceilings as shown in figure 9.8. These can be used as a thermally insulated ceiling beneath an uninsulated roof space or as an inclined roof construction, for example under a green roof. The first loadbearing straw bale vaults with a building permit were built in Germany in 2013 at Buchberg-Wangelin (p. 138).

9.1 Straw bale dome for a sound studio, Forstmehren, Germany, 2003 (Design: Gernot Minke, Friedemann Mahlke)

9.2, 9.3 Straw bale barrel vault for a holiday residence, Bad Schussenried, Germany, 2007 (Design: Gernot Minke).

9.4

9.5

9.6

9.9

– Ventilated roof
– Wooden floorboards or OSB board
– Timber battens
– Earth mortar levelling
– Straw bales cut at an angle
– Earth plaster (several coats)

– Plant substrate
– Roofing membrane
– Earth mortar levelling
– Straw bales cut at an angle
– Earth plaster (vapour-retarding,
  several coats)

Conically cut bales,
stacked in the form
of an inverted
catenary curve

9.7

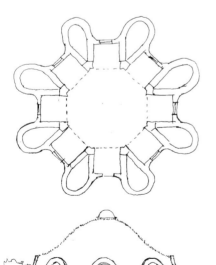

9.8

9.4 Cutting apparatus, FEB, 2007

9.5 Improved cutting apparatus, FEB, 2009

9.6 Housing units made of loadbearing straw bale barrel vaults, Tamera, Portugal, 2007 (Design: Gernot Minke)

9.7 Straw bale layer in the barrel vault

9.8 Plan and elevation for café with loadbearing straw bale dome and barrel vaults (Design: Gernot Minke)

9.9 Straw bale shallow barrel-vaulted ceiling (Design: Benjamin Krick, Gernot Minke)

10   Thermal insulation

Roof insulation

The thermal insulation of roofs with straw bales is in most cases only economically viable if it is considered in detail at the planning stage. A key consideration is that the bales fit easily between the rafters, i.e. that the rafter spacing matches the bale dimensions. If the spacing is too narrow, many bales will need shortening. If it is too wide, the gaps will need stuffing with loose straw. Both are very time consuming and therefore uneconomical. If standard small bales (48 × 36 × 70–110 cm) are used, it is particularly economical to choose a rafter spacing that is slightly less than two bales wide, i.e. 94–95 cm. Two bales can then be pressed into place next to each other between the rafters, and bales only need cutting to size at the ridge, around dormers, roof lights and junctions between roof surfaces. Likewise, the height of the rafters should equal the height of the bales (36 cm). To reduce thermal bridging effects and maximise material efficiency, I-section timber beams should be used (10.1).
With this construction, U-values of around $U = 0.15 \, W/(m^2 \cdot K)$ can be achieved. Better U-values are possible using supplementary external insulation or by using larger bales. Figure 10.2 shows a roof construction with sheathing on the inner face beneath the rafters topped with a vapour barrier, for example of polyethylene (PE) foil. The foil also serves as trickle protection, preventing straw particles from falling between joins

in the sheathing. If OSB boards are used as sheathing and the joints are bonded or sealed, there is no need for an additional vapour barrier as OSB boards already exhibit high vapour diffusion resistance (10.1). To achieve a sufficiently fire-retardant structure (with an F30 fire rating), an additional lining of 12.5 mm gypsum fibreboard or plasterboard must be applied to the inner face. Above the straw bales, a vapour permeable membrane or a layer of bituminised softwood fibreboard is placed, followed by counterbattens, battens and the roof covering.
Lower rafter heights can be achieved if the straw bales are arranged above the rafters (10.3). The bales then rest on a layer of sheathing. This construction avoids thermal bridges and the rafter spacing can be independent of the bale dimensions as they are not fitted between the rafters. The roof construction overall is, however, much thicker.
If the bales are positioned above the primary roof structure, the roof covering – i.e. the weatherproof layer – needs to be secured against uplift by wind forces. An additional problem with pitched roofs is the fact that bales tend to slide down leaving a gap at ridge level: they must, therefore, be packed tightly during installation.
These disadvantages can be avoided by choosing a green roof with a sufficiently thick substrate layer (10.3). In this case, the waterproof and root-proof barrier membrane can be laid directly on the

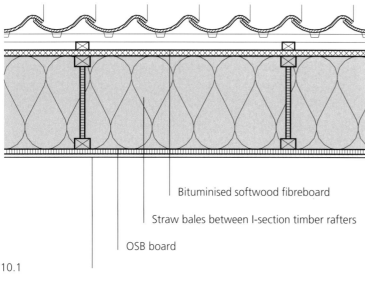

Bituminised softwood fibreboard

Straw bales between I-section timber rafters

OSB board

10.1

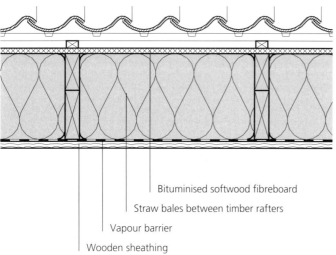

Bituminised softwood fibreboard

Straw bales between timber rafters

Vapour barrier

Wooden sheathing

10.2

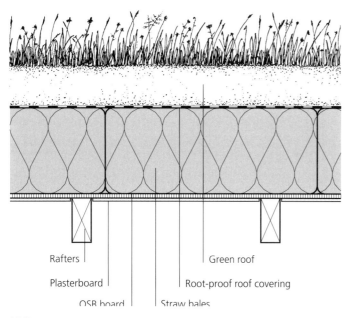

Rafters   Green roof

Plasterboard   Root-proof roof covering

OSB board   Straw bales

10.3

straw bales (For more information on the construction of green roofs, see Minke 2016). As the roof skin of the green roof represents a vapour barrier, it is advisable to install a moisture-adaptive vapour barrier on the underside of the insulation that has a lower vapour-retarding effect at higher humidity levels than at low humidity. This makes it possible for any condensation water that may have diffused into the structure to escape so that the structure can dry out again.

In all solutions, it is advantageous if the straw bale layer is ventilated to allow any residual moisture in the bales or condensation water resulting from inaccurately executed installation of the vapour barrier to dry out *(10.1, 10.2)*.

According to investigations by the Centre for Environmentally Conscious Building (ZUB) at the University of Kassel, the hygrothermal performance of ventilated pitched roof constructions with straw bale insulation is unproblematic if equipped with a vapour barrier on the internal face and a small amount of external insulation, for example in the form of softwood fibreboard (FASBA 2008) *(see chapter 4, p. 26)*. Non-ventilated green roofs with moisture-adaptive vapour barriers were not investigated.

10.1 Roof construction with straw bales between I-section rafters, OSB as stiffening layer and vapour barrier, bituminised softwood fibreboard as external insulation.

10.2 Roof construction with straw bales between rafters, sheathing, vapour barrier, bituminised softwood fibreboard as external insulation.

10.3 Roof construction with exposed rafters, straw bale insulation and green roof.

Floor insulation

Alongside conventional floor constructions, straw bales have been used for the insulation of floors in several straw bale buildings in Europe.

When using straw bales in floors, it is first and foremost essential to ensure that moisture from the ground cannot penetrate the bales, and that the bales are completely dry when installed.

A highly economical solution can be seen in the test building erected in Kassel in 2000/2001 *(pp. 78–81)*. For this building, an approx. 10-cm-thick layer of gravel was poured directly on the ground and covered with an approx. 3-cm-thick layer of sand followed by a PE moisture barrier. On this a layer of recycled timber pallets was placed as a ventilated base for a layer of straw bales. 24 mm OSB boarding was laid directly as a floating floor on the bales – without additional battens –and the joints sealed with 25-mm-wide screwed-down strips of OSB.

A similarly inexpensive floor construction suitable for do-it-yourself construction employs straw bales for the floor insulation (with a vapour barrier on the warm side) that rest on pallets that in turn rest on used car tyres to prevent moisture rising from below.

The strategy of elevating the building to create a thin ventilated cavity under the floor can prove counterproductive according to recent findings: in summer warm, moist air passes beneath the floor and cools down due to the lower temperature of the soil. This increases humidity levels and can lead to condensation and thus to the formation of mould. Inadequately ventilated underfloor cavities are therefore not recommended.

With all floor constructions made with straw bales, it is essential to ensure that any moisture that may penetrate the construction can escape so that it can dry out. As yet, no transient hygrothermal simulations have been carried out for floor constructions.

11   Assembling the straw bale building

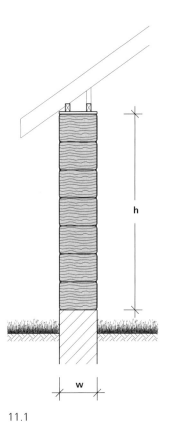

11.1

Loadbearing straw bale walls

As straw bales will be compressed by an imposed load, the following precautions have to be taken for loadbearing straw bale walls:

– The roof load has to be distributed evenly to all walls. Loads must not be concentrated on any spot.
– Roof loads have to be transmitted centrically and have to be distributed over at least 50 % of the wall thickness.
– The ratio of wall height to wall thickness should not go beyond 6:1. If, however, the wall is reinforced by horizontal braces against buckling, the ratio can be exceeded *(11.1)*.
– Straw bales need to be have undamaged stalks, have to be highly compressed and possess a density of at least 110 kg/m³.
– Window openings should be rather narrow – but in any event higher than wide *(11.2)*.
– As far as possible, lintels above windows and doors should be avoided. Instead, the ring beam should be appropriately dimensioned to accommodate this task.
– In case lintels are intended, sufficient tolerance to the ring beam has to be allowed for, as the straw bales tend to creep during the first weeks or months after completion.
– Dimensions between wall openings as well as openings to corners have to equal at least one bale length *(11.2)*.

– For particularly long and slender walls and in the event of very high roof loads, provisions for additional bracing have to be made to avoid buckling.
– Roof loads on the bales should not exceed 20 kN/m².
– Loadbearing walls must be prestressed.
– If walls are not prestressed, a load of 40 kN/m² will cause a settlement of up to 10 % (upright small bales) or up to 14 % (flat small bales). With jumbo bales that have a higher degree of compression, the slump will be less significant.
– Prestressed walls can experience slump as well if the prestressing was insufficient or is reduced over time.

For buildings with loadbearing walls it is better to use large bales as they provide a larger support surface for load distribution and have a higher degree of compression and therefore experience a lower deformation under load. Since thicker wall constructions also have thicker (and therefore more expensive) foundations, it makes sense to use methods of foundation that do not require to reach the frost-free depth of 80–90 cm.
This solution *(11.3)* uses a foam glass gravel layer that acts against the capillary forces and Is located under a thin strip foundation and reaches at least 50 cm outside of the foundation and is at least 30 cm thick.
Figures *11.4–11.6* show options for interesting roof structures ensuring a largely even distribution of forces onto the walls.

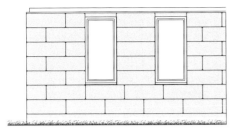

11.2

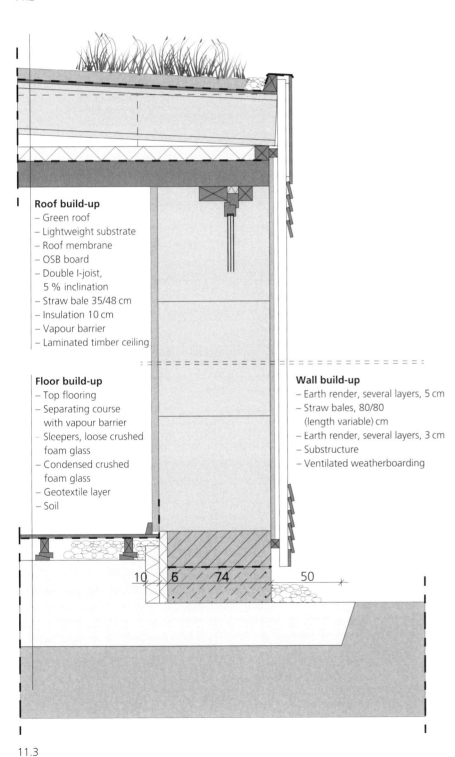

Roof build-up
– Green roof
– Lightweight substrate
– Roof membrane
– OSB board
– Double I-joist,
  5 % inclination
– Straw bale 35/48 cm
– Insulation 10 cm
– Vapour barrier
– Laminated timber ceiling

Floor build-up
– Top flooring
– Separating course
  with vapour barrier
– Sleepers, loose crushed
  foam glass
– Condensed crushed
  foam glass
– Geotextile layer
– Soil

Wall build-up
– Earth render, several layers, 5 cm
– Straw bales, 80/80
  (length variable) cm
– Earth render, several layers, 3 cm
– Substructure
– Ventilated weatherboarding

11.3

11.4

11.5

11.6

11.1 Required wall proportion: w/h ≤ 1/6

11.2 Design of wall openings

11.3 Crushed foam glass layer acting as insulation and water-proofing course

11.4–11.6 Octogonal and square Hogan roofs
(Design: Gernot Minke 1983)

Other suitable forms are pyramidal roofs, whereas common pitched or hipped roofs can cause structural problems. These roof types can only be applied if they are extremely lightweight or if the walls are highly prestressed.

Non-loadbearing straw bale walls

For frame constructions with straw infill panels, the position of posts in relation to the bales has to be considered already at design stage. Figure *11.8* features different possible configurations. If posts are positioned on the interior or exterior of the straw bale layer (positions A and C), the bale length has to be considered only for window and door openings. If the posts are positioned between bales (B and D) the structural grid should be based on the bale length; this would entail equal window and door widths, respectively. The use of latticed posts (D) can be advantageous, as no additional substructure for exterior weatherboarding will be required. Furthermore, the bales fit snugly between the posts, thus providing a relatively even surface. With continuous posts the use of triangle borders is useful to keep bales from dislodging. If bales of different lengths are used and if the structural grid follows primarily structural considerations without regard to bale dimensions, posts should preferably be positioned inside or outside of the straw bale wall: in either case, bales should be laid in a "running bond", avoiding continuous vertical joints *(11.2)*. If supports are positioned outside, that is at the cold exterior side of the wall, they are potentially exposed to the weather, and the insulation level inevitably is penetrated by structural elements. This makes it more difficult to achieve airtightness and may cause thermal bridges. If posts are positioned in cut-out gaps as shown in figure *11.8*, solution E, this can create a better base for interior lining, reduce the overall wall thickness and facilitate the fixing of shelves or wall cabinets. Figure *11.7* pictures such a gap that was cut out with a chain saw.

It is advisable to use the bales in an on-end position or laid vertically. If the wall is relatively thin, this will result in a better U-value *(see chapter 4, p. 23)*. The following paragraphs will deal with respective structural details of individual wall elements and present detailed drawings of advisable solutions.

Wall build-up in non-loadbearing straw bale walls

Position of the posts

Since the cutting or customising of straw bales is a strenuous procedure, the structural grid and the position and size of wall openings should coincide with the bale dimensions. Furthermore, the position of the posts inside or in front of or behind the bales, as well as the decision as to whether to use simple or composite posts – for instance double T or latticed posts – is of crucial importance for site procedures, detailing and interior fit-out *(11.9–11.11)*. If the straw bales are positioned in front of or behind the primary structure, they must be fixed to it unless the bales are highly prestressed between foundation and ring beam. The position of posts in relation to the surface of the bales bears substantial consequences on the finishing and interior fit-out: if the posts sit flush with the interior face of the bales, an additional plaster base will be required (for example a reed mat). To prevent expansion or shrinkage cracks, for instance caused by timber reacting to humidity, the use of an additional plaster reinforcement mesh is advisable. If the posts are positioned in front of a straw bale wall that is to be plastered, the plastering is time-consuming, as all posts and the connections have to be given a plaster base. Nevertheless, cracks between render and timber are hard to avoid. If the interior is to be lined with gypsum fibreboard, hard fibreboard, OSB, chipboard or plasterboard, the posts should be spaced so that they suit the board dimensions. This also applies to the fixing of an exterior ventilated weatherboarding.

11.7

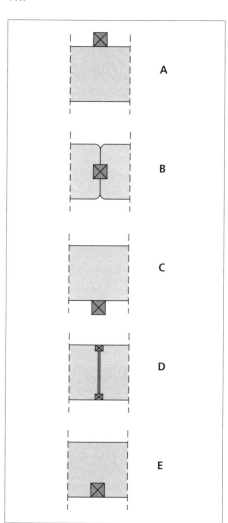

11.8

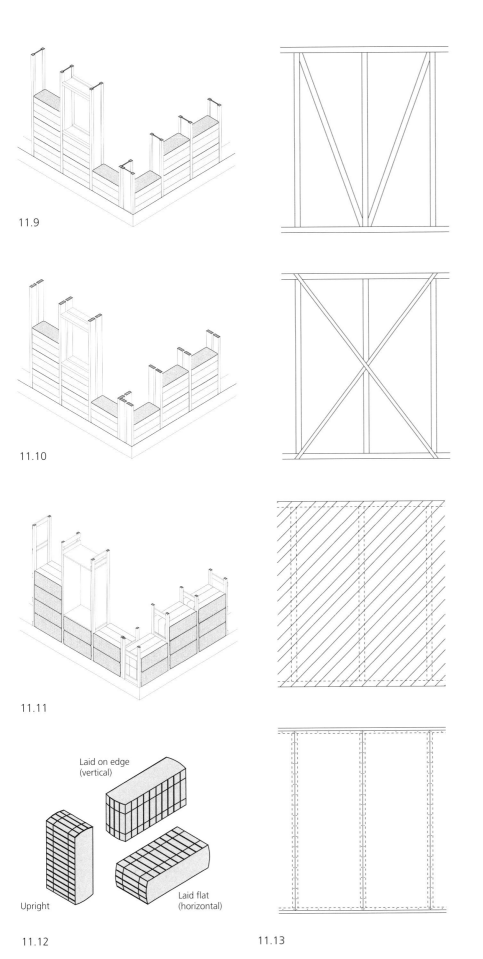

11.9

11.10

11.11

Laid on edge
(vertical)

Upright

Laid flat
(horizontal)

11.12

11.13

11.7 Cut-out gaps for posts

11.8 Potential positions of supports in a wall

11.9 H-profile posts

11.10 Solid timber posts

11.11 Latticed "ladder-type" posts

11.12 Position of the straw bales within the
wall

11.13 Bracing against horizontal forces

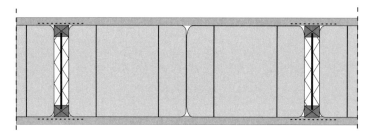

Interior

– Earth plaster (several layers) with
  linseed oil varnish as vapour barrier

– Straw bales

– Lime render (several layers)

Exterior

11.14

Interior

– OSB panel

– Straw bales

– Softwood
  fibreboard

– Render

Exterior

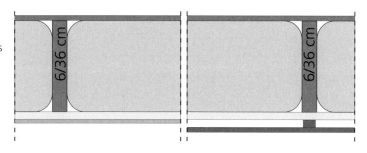

Interior

– OSB panel

– Straw bales

– Softwood fibreboard

– Battens

– Weatherboarding

Exterior

11.15

Interior

– Earth plaster

– Straw bales

– Earth render
  (with weather protection)

Exterior

11.16

Bracing against horizontal forces

As straw bales do not contribute to the stiffening of a wall structure, the timber post-and- beam structure – like any other building – has to be braced against horizontal forces (wind loads). In this context, a construction of individual posts within the bales is a rather difficult solution as the cross-bracings between posts will obstruct installation of the bales. Therefore, composite posts with a width equalling the thickness of the bales are preferred: in this case, bracing is provided by diagonal boarding, steel ribbons or rigid panels like OSB boards *(11.13)*.

Position of straw bales

Straw bales can be installed laid flat (horizontal), laid on edge (vertical) or upright. When installed on edge, the stalks will stand vertical as well, thus providing better thermal insulation (the heat conductivity

coefficient perpendicular to the fibres is lower than the one along the fibres, *see chapter 4, p. 23)* and reducing the wall thickness. However, the rendering of the surfaces is more time-consuming with on-edge bales.

Interconnection of the bales and connection of bales to the loadbearing structure

In non-loadbearing straw bale walls, the straw bales must be connected to the loadbearing structure to avoid dislodging of the bales or buckling of the walls. Constructions with I-joists are apt to hold the bales in place *(11.14)*. Wall constructions with boarding on both sides provide sufficient stability for the bales *(11.15)*. This type of construction can be finished with a plaster on a plaster base or it can be given a weatherboarding or base-top-covering. With box girders or massive timber posts,

triangle borders on the inside and outside of the supports will keep the bales from dislodging *(11.16)*.

In a loadbearing straw construction, the bales have to be connected with each other, with the foundation and the ring beam. In addition to this, the building regulations of New Mexico, USA, stipulate another option for the construction of non-loadbearing straw bale walls: the straw bales should be placed between the timber posts and connected to them by expanded metal angles. The lowest two bale layers must be tied to the foundation via steel rods with at least two rods per one bale. Additionally, the upper bale layers must be interconnected with steel rods *(11.17)*. These provisions are very labour-intensive and might – under European climatic conditions – assist condensation on the steel rods and thus potentially result in damages to the building. After all, these rods are not required if

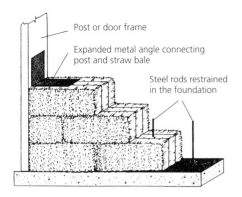

Post or door frame

Expanded metal angle connecting post and straw bale

Steel rods restrained in the foundation

11.17

11.18

bales are prestressed between foundation or grade beam and ring beam. The pre-stressing will create sufficient friction at the joints between bales and between bales and loadbearing structure, usually making additional connections unnecessary.

Wall corners

In the case of loadbearing straw bale walls, the bales should interlock at the corners or be held in place by the posts for structural reasons; interlocking walls will reinforce each other against horizontal forces and will not buckle at the open ends. Figure *11.18* illustrates how doors and windows can provide bracing for the walls. At freestanding corners with interlocking bale layers it is advisable to connect the layers with sticks running vertically through two and half bales. Since it is difficult to thread the sticks through jumbo bales with their higher density, steel rods with U-shaped hooks can be used in this case.

Foundations, bases and connection to floor

The type of foundation of a building will – above all – depend on the frost line and loadbearing capabilities of the ground. In the particular case of straw bale walls,

their relatively great thickness entails larger – and therefore more expensive – foundations. One solution to bypass this problem may be the provision of a beam supported by point foundations, as shown in *11.21*. As the test building discussed in *chapter 14, pp. 78–81*, shows, this is also an economical solution. Another financially viable method may be the construction of strip foundations out of locally resourced natural stone or recycled bricks – provided the owners build them on their own account. Yet another cost-effective solution may be the construction of a floating floor slab on an insulation layer of crushed foam glass *(11.19)*. The crushed glass layer consists of recycled glass in a size range of 0 to 90 mm. The layer is compacted with a vibrator, and in a highly compacted state it has a heat conductivity of $0.08\,W/(m\cdot K)$ whereas in a loose state the value is $0.06\,W/(m\cdot K)$. In this build-up the closed cells of the foamed glass intercept capillary action. However, a waterproofing course against vapour and possibly radon should be included as well. It is important that thermal bridges in the foundation and base area are avoided. A rather unconventional but very economical do-it-yourself solution is the use of disposed car tyres filled with lean concrete: the tyres can be resourced free of charge from petrol stations or car

11.14 Stabilising of bales by adequate positioning of posts (horizontal section)

11.15 Wall with boarding on both sides, plastered (left) and rear-ventilated (right)

11.16 Stabilising of bales by adequate positioning of post with triangle borders

11.17 Bale connection according to New Mexico Code

11.18 Bracing of the wall with windows and doors

11.19 Base with crushed foam glass layer acting as insulation and water-proofing course

11.20 Base with lightweight vertically perforated bricks

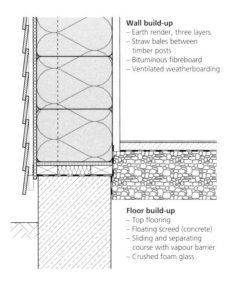

Wall build-up
– Earth render, three layers
– Straw bales between timber posts
– Bituminous fibreboard
– Ventilated weatherboarding

Floor build-up
– Top flooring
– Floating screed (concrete)
– Sliding and separating course with vapour barrier
– Crushed foam glass

11.19

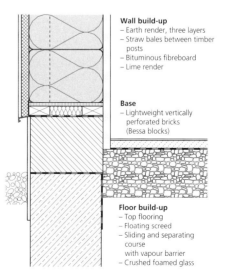

Wall build-up
– Earth render, three layers
– Straw bales between timber posts
– Bituminous fibreboard
– Lime render

Base
– Lightweight vertically perforated bricks (Bessa blocks)

Floor build-up
– Top flooring
– Floating screed
– Sliding and separating course with vapour barrier
– Crushed foamed glass

11.20

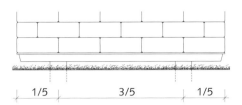

1/5	3/5	1/5

11.21

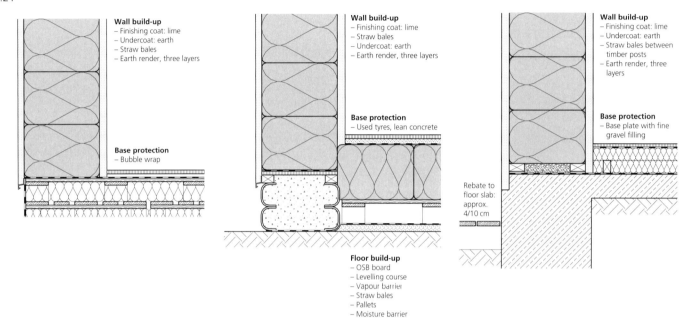

Wall build-up
– Finishing coat: lime
– Undercoat: earth
– Straw bales
– Earth render, three layers

Base protection
– Bubble wrap

11.22

Wall build-up
– Finishing coat: lime
– Straw bales
– Undercoat: earth
– Earth render, three layers

Base protection
– Used tyres, lean concrete

Floor build-up
– OSB board
– Levelling course
– Vapour barrier
– Straw bales
– Pallets
– Moisture barrier

11.23

Wall build-up
– Finishing coat: lime
– Undercoat: earth
– Straw bales between timber posts
– Earth render, three layers

Base protection
– Base plate with fine gravel filling

Rebate to floor slab: approx. 4/10 cm

11.24

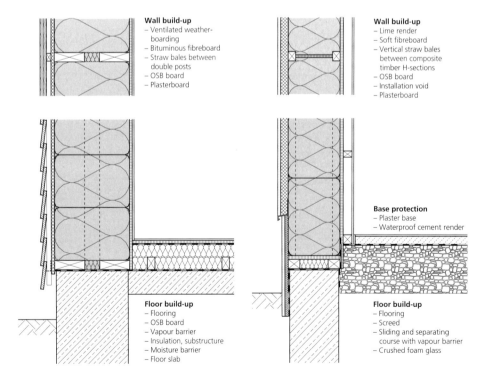

Wall build-up
– Ventilated weatherboarding
– Bituminous fibreboard
– Straw bales between double posts
– OSB board
– Plasterboard

Floor build-up
– Flooring
– OSB board
– Vapour barrier
– Insulation, substructure
– Moisture barrier
– Floor slab

11.25

Wall build-up
– Lime render
– Soft fibreboard
– Vertical straw bales between composite timber H-sections
– OSB board
– Installation void
– Plasterboard

Base protection
– Plaster base
– Waterproof cement render

Floor build-up
– Flooring
– Screed
– Sliding and separating course with vapour barrier
– Crushed foam glass

11.26

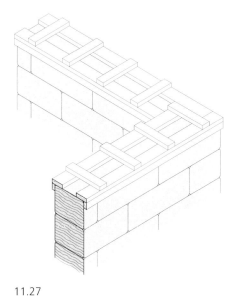

11.27

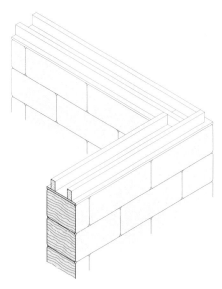

11.28

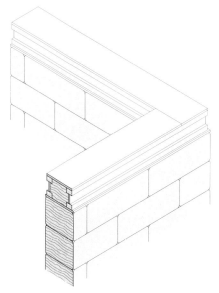

11.29

11.21 Structurally optimised positioning of point foundations

11.22 Base consisting of pallets

11.23 Base consisting of recycled car tyres

11.24 Base detail with gravel course and rebate to accommodate render layer

11.25 Wall-floor junction with insulation on concrete slab (top horizontal section, below vertical section)

11.26 Wall-floor junction with foam glass gravel (top horizontal section, below vertical section)

11.27 Ring beam as composite ladder-type element

11.28 Ring beam with bottom boards for load distribution

11.29 Boxed ring beam made of composite timber H-sections

tyre dealers, and the amount of required concrete will be low if demolition rubbish and rocks are used as aggregate *(11.23)*. Besides providing a splash skirting for the straw bale wall, a base or plinth has to fulfil numerous tasks: it has to be waterproof, pressure-proof and intercept capillary action, and must also provide sufficient thermal insulation. These requirements can be met with lightweight Bessa blocks (lightweight vertically perforated bricks) with an exterior layer of waterproof render *(11.20)*. However, as this render acts as a vapour barrier the base should receive an interior vapour-proof finish as well. In the event that interior spaces are flooded, water may soak the straw bales: thus, it is advisable to start the first layer of straw bales a few centimetres above the finished floor level *(11.20)*. Figures *11.22* and *11.23* show experimental do-it-yourself solutions using used pallets and tyres. It has to be made sure that voids and cavities of the pallets are filled with insulating material like polystyrene pellets and that they are coated with waterproof material like bubble wrap. The car tyres can be filled with lean concrete. Figure *11.24* shows a solution from Australia by Frank Thomas: here, a rebate in the floor slab at a height of approx. 10 cm accommodates the exterior render to prevent cracking as a result

of sagging of the render. Floor planks lift the bales slightly and facilitate the threading of tensioning wires for prestressing of the walls. A crushed stone or gravel bed under the bales traps condensate that might otherwise assist decay of the bales. The bales should not directly touch a foil or a bituminous fibreboard for this reason. Humidity must always diffuse back into the room. The detailing of the lower junction of wall and foundation and floor must ensure that there are no thermal bridges and that the straw and earth render in that area is protected from splash water. Figures *11.25* and *11.27* show some possible solutions.

Ring beams

The ring beam – that is, the upper wall junction – will perform multiple tasks: it receives the roof loads and distributes them evenly over the entire wall length; it stabilises the top course of straw bales and, hence, prevents buckling of the entire wall. It reinforces bracing of the wall corners and can also function as a lintel to door and window openings, provided they are not too big. Therefore, the ring beam has to be particularly bending-resistant or rigid and as wide as possible. Composite, ladder-type ring beams were found to be a preferable and economical solution for the even distri-

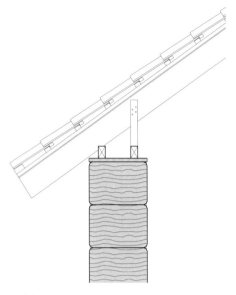

11.30

11.31

11.32

bution of roof loads *(11.27).* Other options for the distribution of loads are chipboards or OSB boards, which are fixed underneath the actual ring beams *(11.28).* Lightweight ring beams with a high loadbearing capacity can be assembled out of composite timber H-sections *(11.29).* In any event, roof loads have to be transmitted in the centre of the ring beam and the wall. Figure *11.30* shows a solution that meets this requirement even with a steep roof. Great care has to be taken to avoid thermal bridges. Usually, ring beams are made of wood. There are built examples made of steel and reinforced concrete: however, they are usually not suitable for the Northern and Central European climates as they require relatively complicated insulation details to avoid thermal bridges.

Windows and doors

Position and design of window and door junctions are of crucial importance to avoid damages to the building. The following discussion will concentrate on windows only since both windows and doors involve the same design issues. To reduce thermal bridges, the exterior surface of the window frames should be covered by insulation *(11.33–11.36).*

The deeper the window is recessed into the wall, the higher the shading by reveal and overhang. Besides that, snow and ice deposits can build on a deep window sill causing higher risks of moisture damages. The junction between window frame and exterior render is critical as water can easily penetrate here. This can be avoided by using a cover strip with a sealing tape behind it or by integrating an elastic maintenance joint. The reveals corner can be reinforced with a plaster rail which results in a sharp angle *(11.33)* or the corner can be rounded *(11.35).* Round or chamfered corners result in the admittance of more daylight in the interior and create a more pleasant, gentle transition of light levels. In the wall with exterior timber cladding build-up in *11.34* it is possible to replace the exterior softwood fibreboard by a thin earth plaster.

Figure *11.36* shows a solution where the window soffit was not rendered but built from timber panels.

A careful connection of the airtight layer is crucial for the functioning of the window and for avoiding structural damage. For the junction between window frame and plaster there are special connection tapes that are adhesive to the frame on the one side and are plastered over on the other side. These tapes are fleece-covered to achieve a good plaster base. Special adhesive tapes also exist for connecting window frames and timber panels. Another option is to glue window frame and timber panel together as part of the prefabrication process. In this case, the pre-assembled window reveal panel is connected with the airtight layer of the building with an adhesive tape.

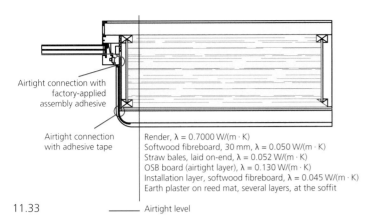

Airtight connection with
factory-applied
assembly adhesive

Airtight connection
with adhesive tape

Render, λ = 0.7000 W/(m · K)
Softwood fibreboard, 30 mm, λ = 0.050 W/(m · K)
Straw bales, laid on-end, λ = 0.052 W/(m · K)
OSB board (airtight layer), λ = 0.130 W/(m · K)
Installation layer, softwood fibreboard, λ = 0.045 W/(m · K)
Earth plaster on reed mat, several layers, at the soffit

11.33 ——— Airtight level

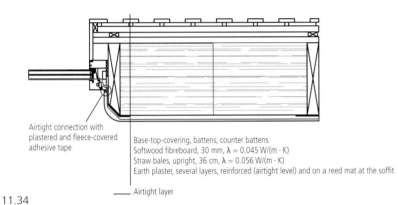

Airtight connection with
plastered and fleece-covered
adhesive tape

Base-top-covering, battens, counter battens
Softwood fibreboard, 30 mm, λ = 0.045 W/(m · K)
Straw bales, upright, 36 cm, λ = 0.056 W/(m · K)
Earth plaster, several layers, reinforced (airtight level) and on a reed mat at the soffit

—— Airtight layer

11.34

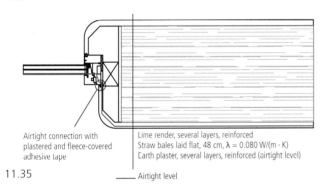

Airtight connection with
plastered and fleece-covered
adhesive tape

Lime render, several layers, reinforced
Straw bales laid flat, 48 cm, λ = 0.080 W/(m · K)
Earth plaster, several layers, reinforced (airtight level)

—— Airtight level

11.35

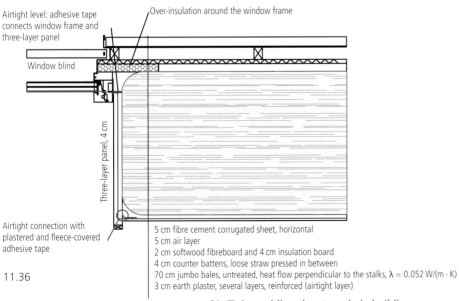

Airtight level: adhesive tape
connects window frame and
three-layer panel

Over-insulation around the window frame

Window blind

Three-layer panel, 4 cm

Airtight connection with
plastered and fleece-covered
adhesive tape

11.36

5 cm fibre cement corrugated sheet, horizontal
5 cm air layer
2 cm softwood fibreboard and 4 cm insulation board
4 cm counter battens, loose straw pressed in between
70 cm jumbo bales, untreated, heat flow perpendicular to the stalks, λ = 0.052 W/(m · K)
3 cm earth plaster, several layers, reinforced (airtight layer)

11.30 Central transmission of loads with a
steep pitched roof

11.31, 11.32 Installation of windows

11.33 Window connection detail with I-joist
and bales laid on end

11.34 Window connection detail in a wooden
plank wall, bales laid on end

11.35 Window connection detail with loadbearing straw bale wall, bales laid flat

11.36 Window connection detail with jumbo
bales

Wall and roof junctions

Wall and roof junctions should prevent the formation of thermal bridges. If the exterior surfaces are rendered, a sufficient roof overhang should be provided as a protection against driving rain. Ventilated exterior weatherboarding must prevent snow or pelting rain from meeting the exposed or earth-rendered surface of the straw bales. Figures *11.37–11.40* show various solutions for these tasks. The junction detail of roof rafters has to ensure that loads are transmitted in the centre of the ring beam to avoid torsion.

Interior walls

The construction of straw bale partitions does not make much sense: unlike conventional partitions they require wide foundations and increase the cubical contents of the building. Furthermore, straw bale buildings provide relatively little thermal mass and it is advisable to build interior walls from solid bricks, possibly even natural stone. The most favourable material for the indoor climate are unfired earth bricks that have a high heat storage capacity and – more than other solid building materials – have the capability to regulate air humidity *(see chapter 4, p. 24)*.

Intermediate ceilings

Intermediate ceilings in two-storey straw bale buildings are usually wooden joist or stacked plank ceilings. They have to ensure proper air-borne and footfall sound insulation. Figure *11.41* shows a simple ceiling and floor build-up that is largely suitable for do-it-yourself construction: earth bricks positioned in-between the ceiling and floor

layers improve air-borne sound insulation, provide thermal mass and balance air humidity. An entirely different but advantageous solution are vertically stacked planks *(11.42)*: here, a solid timber ceiling is formed by vertical closely stacked boards fixed together with nails or dowels. The advantage here is the low construction height and the good air-borne sound insulation without the need for additional structural measures. Furthermore, this ceiling type can be entirely or at least largely prefabricated, which allows fast installation – provided that a crane is used.

Service ducts

If possible, water pipes should not run inside straw bale walls; cold water pipes assist condensation leading to the soaking of the bales. In theory, this should not be a problem for hot water pipes, provided they are fully enclosed by the straw without any gaps or openings at joints as is often the case in reality. A further disadvantage is the fact that leaks are hard to detect. Therefore, pipes should be integrated into the floor or stud walls, behind skirting boards or they should be simply installed on top of the walls *(11.43)*. The same rules apply for electrical wires. If wires penetrate the straw layer, they have to be encased in a non-inflammable conduit or tubes. Sockets and switches are best integrated into door frames or on columns. If they need to be fixed where no timber backing is provided, it has to be ensured that they are firmly back-fixed to a batten or wedge hammered into the straw bale or they could be fastened to a post with gypsum. US building codes stipulate that electrical wires have to be encased with a 3-cm-thick mortar layer to minimise the risk of fire.

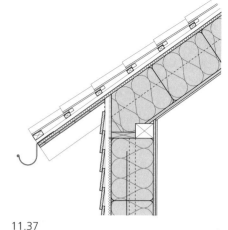

11.37

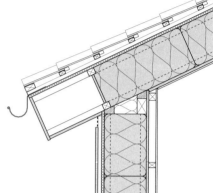

11.38

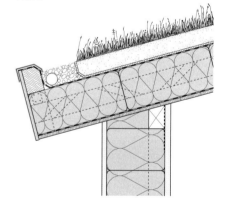

11.39

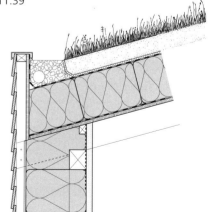

11.40

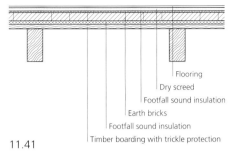

11.41

Flooring
Dry screed
Footfall sound insulation
Earth bricks
Footfall sound insulation
Timber boarding with trickle protection

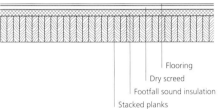

11.42

Flooring
Dry screed
Footfall sound insulation
Stacked planks

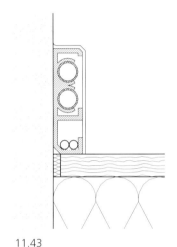

11.43

11.37 Roof-wall junction with post-and-beam-construction

11.38 Roof-wall junction with I-joists

11.39 Roof-wall junction with rafters

11.40 Roof-wall junction with top-of-roof insulation

11.41 Wooden joist floor

11.42 Vertically stacked plank floor

11.43 Skirting with integrated heating pipes and wiring

11.44 Wall niche with lamp

11.45 Integrated wall lamps (design: Manfred Fahnert)

11.46 Wall niche

11.47 Light opening

11.48 Straw viewing wall opening

11.44

11.47

Heavy-duty fixings in straw ball walls

If the interior finish consists simply of plaster on the bales, an appropriate substructure has to be provided to enable the fixing of shelving, hanging cupboards, wall-mounted lights, heavy paintings and other fixtures. In most cases, this is not required if the interior is clad with timber, MDF or OSB boards. For the flexible fixing of pictures, a simple wooden batten (picture rail) may be provided on the top end of the wall.

11.45

11.46

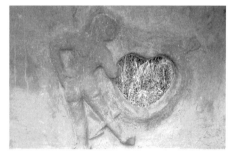

11.48

Wall recesses

Straw bale walls provide the chance for creative sculptural wall design, as recesses for shelving, pictures or lights can be easily cut into the thick walls (11.44–11.47). However, recesses can create thermal bridges. Often a spot in the wall is intentionally exposed to reveal the straw inside the wall (11.48).

12   Surface protection and finishing works

12.1

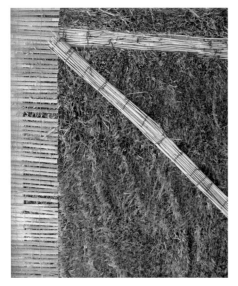

12.2

General rules

Plastering of straw bale surfaces is the simplest way of interior finishing. The plaster hardens and smoothes the bale surface and provides airtightness and fire protection. At all joints between two different materials, at edges and for large areas, the plaster should be reinforced by a tensile mesh to prevent cracking. Suitable products are earth, stucco, lime, cement and lime-cement Plaster. Cement plasters are not recommended because of their brittleness and their low elasticity. Basically earth plasters are suitable for most inner surfaces as they contribute to balancing the humidity in the interior more than any other plaster. Earth renders can be used on the exterior only on weather-protected areas. In regions with minimal rain, stabilised earth renders are an option. As a rule, however, lime renders are more suitable. It is usually important to plaster the straw bale walls from the inside first so that the moisture can diffuse outwards relatively unhindered. If the interior plaster is applied after the exterior render, there is a risk of moisture condensing outside on the straw which might lead to the formation of mould. This is especially the case in the cold season. However, the first thin layer of earth plaster that only serves fire protection can be applied without risk.

Earth plaster

Due to its elasticity and its ability to balance air humidity, earth plaster has a substantial advantage over all other plaster materials. As discussed earlier in *chapter 4, p. 26* – sorption and humidity regulation – earth plaster evidently absorbs more moisture at a given high air humidity than other plaster materials and vice versa. Usually, plaster is applied in three layers: the undercoat smoothes the bale surface and immerses sticking-out stalks. This layer should be applied with high pressure and is best sprayed on with a pump. The plaster should be rather liquid to penetrate a few centimetres beyond the surface. Stalk ends are smoothed over with a board or a trowel *(12.1)*. It is also possible to rub the plaster into the bale surface by hand. The earth plaster should possess a high clay content to ensure strong adhesion to the straw stalks. The first layer will tend to creep and leave cracks as it dries: this is not hazardous, but rather increases adhesion of the top coats. Timber profiles need to be given a plaster base, for instance reed or bamboo *(12.2)*. Subsequent cracking due to expansion or shrinking of the wood can be avoided by incorporating a plaster base with sufficient overlap in the plaster itself. The second coat has to be leaner or, in in other words, the contents of additives like sand and fine gravel need to be increased to reduce cracking during the drying process. Further suitable additives are saw dust or straw chaff, hemp, sisal, flax or coconut fibres and ground straw. These fibres act as a reinforcement at the same time. The main task of this coat is to roughly level the surface and prepare it for the top coat. Holes and uneven areas with a depth of more than 2 cm should be levelled with a mixture of chaff and earth before applying the second coat. The finishing coat is 5 to 10 mm thick and forms the outer skin. Coarse sand, milled straw chaff, grain fibres or similar materials can be added to the earth to prevent cracking or improve the appearance. In this case, the contents of adhesive clay are to be reduced to 5 to 8 %. Therefore, it is important that the second coat is well moistened and, if needed, roughened up for better adhesion of the final coat. The plaster should be firmly thrown on and levelled.

After initial drying, this final coat can be treated with a moist felt or sponge to create a rough finish of exposed coarse additives such as sand and straw. The individual coats amount to an overall thickness of 3 to 6 cm. Generally speaking, the thermal insulation provided by the wall and the positive effects on air humidity will be the better the thicker the overall plaster coat is.

Other types of plaster

To increase the strength or integrity of the plastered surface, the render coats can also be finished off with a lime top coat. In such an event, it is advisable to integrate a tension- proof reinforcement mesh. For further information on lime render, see *p. 66*. Compared to earth plaster, cement plaster is fairly brittle and cracks will develop more easily as a result of movements of the substructure, wind loads or creeping of the bales. They should therefore be reinforced with glass fibre or metal meshes. Performance in terms of vapour diffusion and humidity balance is less favourable (Minke 2001) than that of earth plaster *(12.3)*. Gypsum plaster is the material least favourable in terms of humidity balance and heat storage, and therefore it will not be discussed here in further detail.

Exterior render

General rules

Exterior render materials have to prevent moisture from entering the straw bales and should, on the other hand, be vapour-permeable so that condensate can diffuse to the outside. However, exterior renders on straw bale walls that are exposed to rain are problematic, because driving rain and capillary action can create a critical level of humidity in the straw. Therefore rendered surfaces must be protected from rain. The most effective way to achieve this is the use of boarding. If an exposed rendered surface is desired, rain protection has to be provided otherwise. Large roof overhangs, green façades, vegetation in front of the façade or protection from a neighbouring building are options in this respect. It might be possible to use earth render or stabilised

12.1 Smoothing of the undercoat with a wooden board

12.2 A plaster base of bamboo and reed allows the plastering of the timber posts

12.3 Vapour diffusion coefficient of various types of plaster

12.3

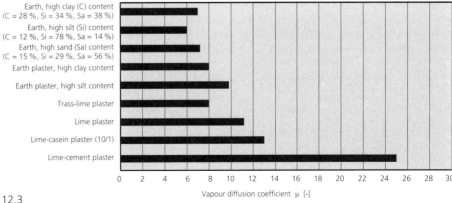

earth render on façades not located on the weather side of a building. Generally speaking, however, a lime render is to be preferred.

Earth plasters

Earth render is only suitable for exterior use if it is protected from rain or if additives or paint coats increase its water resistance. Paint coats like linseed oil, varnish or latex, however, will substantially reduce vapour diffusion (12.10). They act as a vapour barrier and may lead to the collection of damaging condensation water within the bales, provided that the interior build-up does not include a vapour barrier or vapour-resistant paint coat. A cement coat on top of an earth coat easily leads to damages: cement render is much less elastic than earth render, which may cause fissures under thermal or mechanical impact. If water penetrates those fissures, the earth will expand and chip off the top coat; this process may even be exacerbated by frost. In this context, lime render tends to cause far fewer problems, provided that cracks in the surface can be avoided.

Stabilised earth plasters

Stabilised earth plasters contain, in addition to earth, other mineral or organic binding agents such as lime, cement, gypsum, modified starch, methyl cellulose, cow manure, oils, resins, bitumen emulsion or synthetic binders. After curing they are no longer dissolvable in water. Stabilised exterior renders can be applied to building areas with low rain load. For earth plasters stabilised against humidity with linseed oil or bitumen emulsion, one has to bear in mind that they have a strong vapour barrier effect and that therefore are not suitable for climatic zones with large seasonal temperature fluctuations. The ideal quantity of additives depends on the composition of the earth and should always be tested before use. Advantageous mixtures, which have been tested successfully by the author

in a temperate climate in Colombia are described in figure 12.5. It was found that the earth mixtures with linseed oil varnish and with lime/cement were harder to mix and process as the other mixtures. The addition of 6 % bitumen emulsion paste resulted in the best rain resistance, however, the plaster absorbed some water after a very long rain which reduced the compressive strength. The wheat flour paste was produced according to the following recipe: 1 part flour is mixed with 1 part cold water, then stirred lump-free and diluted with 2 parts boiling water. This pulp is kept simmering until it becomes almost transparent. If a mixture of cow dung and earth is used, it is important that the paste is kept wet for several days to allow sufficient fermenting. This increases the abrasion resistance and the resistance against rain. Figure 12.4 shows the results of driving rain tests and abrasion tests, which were carried out Research Laboratory for Experimental Building (FEB) at the University of Kassel on stabilised earth plasters (Minke 2009). The driving rain simulation demonstrated that the non-stabilised pure earth plaster already showed visible erosion after three seconds, while no erosion occurred on some of the stabilised plasters even after six days of water jet treatment. It is interesting to compare the different surface strengths against mechanical abrasion; the right side of figure 12.4 shows the various abrasion quantities in grams.

Lime render

Lime render, which is sometimes also used in conjunction with cement as an additive, is a reliable exterior render material. It is of great importance that the bale surface is smoothed and all cavities and dents are filled beforehand with light clay mixed with straw. One should be aware of some details of the setting of lime render: it reacts with the carbon dioxide from the air to eventually form the compound $CaCO_3$. This process is very slow and takes place only in a moist environment; hence, at the first stage, the

render must not dry out completely and needs to be protected from strong sunlight and – if required – needs to be watered. During the first weeks, it also has to be protected from pelting rain since at this stage it is easily washed off. Although setting is largely finished after three months, lime render reaches its final hardness only after three years. It is advisable to add an extra 5 % of cement to speed up setting through hydraulic binding. The same goes for trass-lime render, which is also a hydraulic binder. The undercoat should be applied with high pressure and is best sprayed on with a pump so that the stalks get fully immersed. The following two coats can be applied under use of a plaster base (reed mat or metal mesh). The plaster base can be omitted but in any event a reinforcement mesh should be integrated into the second coat to prevent fissures. The final coat must not include any fissures. Micro-fissures of 0.2 mm or less can be painted over. Splash water protection is a crucial requirement and can be provided by means of water-repellent additives or paint coats, or a splash skirting. Lime render is made up of 1 part lime and 3 to 4 parts sand. The lime can be used in the form of slaked lime (calcium hydroxide) or – as builders often recommend – stored wet-slaked lime that is produced by soaking lime pieces for months or years. This process is basically the storing of a soggy mass of slaked lime; over time, the heavier, coarser components will form a deposit on the bottom producing extremely smooth stuff at the top. After setting, this lime putty possesses a high elasticity. Also commercially available slaked lime should better be soaked for a number of days before being used as render. The coarser lime deposits on the bottom should be used only as mortar for brickwork. Lime render reacts strongly alkaline. Therefore it should be processed only with protective gloves and protective goggles must be worn. Publications dealing with the restoration of timber-framed houses often recommend trass-lime render instead of pure lime render. This render consists of an undercoat

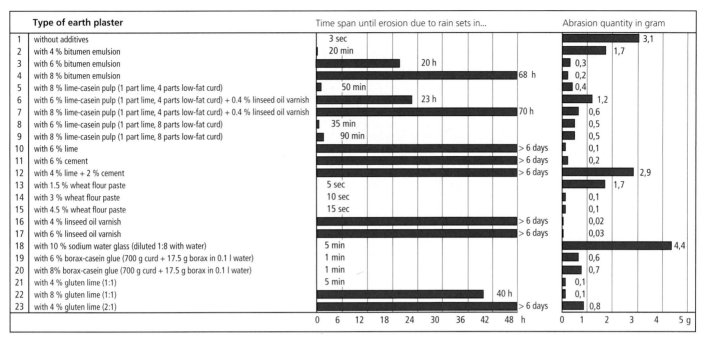

12.4

Type of earth plaster		First layer	Second layer [1]	First layer	Second layer	First layer	Second layer	First layer	Second layer	First layer	Second layer	First layer	Second layer
Clayey loam, masoned				2	2	1	1	1	1	1	1	1	1
Coarse sand (0–4 mm)		1.5	1	3	3	1	0.5	1.5	1.5	1.5	1	1.5	1.5
Fine sand (0–1 mm)		1	1	1	1	1	1.5	1	1.5	1	1.5	1	1
Moist cow dung, mixed 1:1 with clay pudding, fermented		1	1	1	1							0.5	1
Lime										5%	5%		
Cement										5%	5%		
Bitumen emulsion								5%	6%				
Boiled wheat flour paste						3%	4%						
Casein paste mixed with lime 1:1												3%	3%
Linseed oil varnish				4%	4%								
[1] sludge rubbed in with sponge board													

12.5

Plaster no.	Lime powder	Trass-lime	Screed sand	Low-fat curd	Linseed oil varnish	Rich clayey earth	Cow dung	µ value
1	1	–	3	–	–	–	–	11.2
2	–	1	3	–	–	–	–	10.8
3	1	–	6	0.5	–	–	–	6.2
4	1	–	15	0.5	–	3	–	9.7
5	1	–	3	–	0.05	–	–	15.2
6	1	–	3	0.25	0.05	–	–	28.5
7	1.5	–	10	–	–	2	6	8.0

12.6

12.4 Erosion by rain and mechanical abrasion of stabilised earth plasters

12.5 Ingredients (in volume parts) in stabilised earth plasters

12.6 µ values of various types of lime plaster (in volume parts)

of 1 part trass-lime and 3 parts sand and a finishing coat of 1 part trass-lime and 2.5 parts sand. Trass-lime is a highly hydraulic lime consisting of calcium hydrate and trass powder. Hydraulic means that the materials bind water apart from carbon dioxide. There are pros and cons to this kind of render: hydraulic render sets quickly, but is very brittle and does not accommodate to creeping and movements of the wall as does the elastic lime render. For this reason, some builders have ceased to use trass-lime for new straw bale buildings altogether; generally speaking, wet-slaked lime is preferable. To reduce the water absorption of the lime plaster, a casein additive, for example in the form of low-fat curd, is useful. In a compulsory mixer lime and curd can be stirred with water and then sand and gravel is added. Finally, hair or bristles are sprinkled in. Easier to process than animal hair and bristles are coconut fibres. Some builders recommend that, in addition to casein, also some linseed oil varnish is added to the lime plaster; however, this will reduce the water vapour diffusion capacity (12.6). At the Research Laboratory for Experimental Building (FEB), a lime casein plaster with substantially higher casein content was successfully tested as a weatherproof exterior render. It had the ingredients low-fat curd, lime and sand (0–2 mm) in a mixture of 1 : 10 : 40 volume parts. Using a whisk, the curd cheese must first be mixed with the lime without addition of water to a thick-creamy paste. However, one has to bear in mind the reduced water vapour diffusion capacity of these plasters. For repairing cracks and as thin painting plaster, which is applied with a wide brush (tassel), an even richer mixture has been proven useful: low-fat curd, lime, sand (0–1 mm) in a mixture of 1 : 6 : 25 volume parts. In warm countries, often some salt is added to the lime plaster. This has the effect of keeping the plaster moist longer and thus the lime sets faster and better. In Germany, herring brine was formerly used as an additive, which, due to its high salt content has a similar effect. In addition to that,

the proteins contained in the herring brine have a minor stabilising effect. The FEB also tested to what extent the adding of linseed oil varnish and and low-fat curd will reduce the water vapour diffusion capacity of lime plasters. The thus determined µ values (Minke 2001) are shown in figure 12.6.

Lime top coats on earth undercoat

When a lime top coat is applied to an earth undercoat, as is commonly the case with exterior walls, sufficient adhesion between both layers has to be ensured. To achieve this, a coat of acetate of alumina could be applied to the earth undercoat. The first lime coat should have a grain size range up to 6 mm and has to be rubbed hard into the earth coat. Alternatively, a good mechanical bond between both plaster layers can also be achieved by raking holes into the damp earth surface or by using a scraper to create narrow grooves (12.7).

Plaster edges

With any window great care has to be taken to avoid a direct connection between exterior plaster and window sill. Due to the inevitable joint there water can penetrate the plaster by capillary action which can result in flaking off of the plaster, mould formation and damages due to frost (12.8). In this case the metal sheet must be pulled up sideways or, in the case of a wooden window sill, a marginal profile needs to be built in (12.9).

Paint coats

Exposed paint coats are deteriorated by mechanical forces like wind and frost and by chemical forces like ultraviolet radiation and acidic rain and have to be regularly renewed. Exterior paint coats should be water-repellent and at the same time permeable to allow vapour diffusion. Moisture that penetrates the wall as a result of pelting rain or condensation has to be able to escape to the outside. For this reason,

12.7

12.8

12.9

latex, synthetic and emulsion (oil) paints are less suitable for this kind of use. To which degree paint coats can hinder water vapour diffusion was tested by Research Laboratory for Experimental Building (FEB) at the University of Kassel (Minke 2001); the results are shown in figure *12.10*. The diffusion-equivalent air layer thickness (s_d) of various paint types is indicated in metres in this figure. s_d represents the thickness of an air layer equivalent to the thickness of a coat with the same vapour diffusion coefficient. The vapour diffusion coefficient equals the diffusion-equivalent air-layer thickness of a coat divided by the thickness of the coat or layer:

$$\mu = s_d / s$$

A high s_d value means that the resistance against vapour diffusion is high. The following paragraphs discuss a number of tried and tested paints.

Pure lime whitewash

When preparing a whitewash, it has to be observed that the lime mix is fairly fluid; this will not cover up the render colour in one coat, however; rich covering and lime wash coats tend to chip off after drying.

It is advisable to apply three to four thin coats. The mix should be made up of one 50-kg bag of calcium hydrate dissolved in 50 to 60 litres of water. Approx. 1 to 2 kg of common salt should be added to keep the paint coat moist as long as possible to speed up setting. In warmer climates, common salt is often added to lime render as salt binds water and assists setting. As mentioned before, herring brine was used in the old days because of its high salt content. This brine also contains stabilising proteins and – as in lime-casein paint – assists the formation of non-water soluble calcium albuminate. The first coat should be particularly thin so that the lime milk can penetrate the earth render finishing coat. Lime whitewash results in bright white surfaces. To tone the mixture down, fine clay powder or other earth colour pigments are suitable for use with lime. Under Middle European climatic conditions, an exterior lime whitewash will last approx. two to four years; pure lime whitewash is not wipe-resistant.

Lime-casein paint coat
Lime paint coats will get more durable and wipe-resistant when whey, non-fat curd or casein powder is added to the mixture. Non-fat curd contains about 11 % of

casein. Lime and casein react chemically and form the compound calcium albuminate. Historic lime whitewashes are often a mixture of slaked lime putty, non-fat milk or whey. A tested and tried mixture ratio is 1 part non-fat curd, 1 to 3 parts lime and 1.5 to 2.5 parts of water. If linseed oil varnish is added at a maximum of 10 % of the curd contents, it will make the mixture more resistant to wiping but also more difficult to handle. The linseed oil has to be mixed in very carefully, ideally with a whisk, to create a smooth emulsion. To avoid segregation of the mixture and to maintain its consistency, the paint should be stirred occasionally and should be applied within two to four hours; the mixture can be tinted with pigments. (Note that linseed oil varnish reduces vapour diffusion.) In any event, lime-casein coats should be applied to dry surfaces only to prevent formation of moulds. For wet rooms, the following mixture should be used: mix 1 part slaked lime putty with 5 parts non-fat curd for one to two minutes, add 20 parts of lime and mix in with 2 to 4 % linseed oil varnish and – finally – water down. For a wipe-resistant and water-repellent finish, two coats of paint are required; part of the lime can be replaced with pigments suitable for use with lime.

12.7 Earth plaster surface treated with a scraper

12.8 Poor detailing of a plaster edge on a window sill

12.9 Suggested detail of a plaster edge on a hard wood window sill

12.10 s_d-values of various paint products on earth render

Finishing coats to earth plaster with high clay contents	
Lime, two layers	
Chalk-glue, two layers	
Lime-casein (1/8)*, two layers	
Lime-casein (1/1)*, two layers	
Non-fat curd (German quark), one layer	
Sodium-water solution, one layer	
Lime-casein linseed oil, two layers	
Water-based silica paint, two layers	
Emulsion paint, two layers	
Beeswax paint, two layers	
Latex paint, two layers	
Linseed oil varnish, one layer	
Impregnations of earth plaster with high clay contents	
BS 15, Wacker, two layers	
Baysilone, Bayer, two layers	
Façade impregnation, Herbol, two layers	
Stone proofer H, Wacker, two layers	

*Denotes mixture ratio in volume parts

Diffusion-equivalent air layer thickness s_d [m]

12.10

Borax-casein paint coats

Instead of lime, casein can also be mixed with borax (a complex borate mineral) forming a non-water soluble compound comparable to the lime-casein mixture. If the borax content is too high, it will crystallise and impair the visual appearance of the finish. Borax is colour-neutral and is therefore very suitable for paint mixtures with coloured additives. The mixture can be condensed and brightened with chalk. Adding clay powder will increase smoothness of the mixture and prevent segregation of the chalk. If casein powder is used instead of curd, it has to be stored in water for three hours prior to use (320 g casein per 1 litre water). After that, 65 g of Borax is dissolved in 1 litre of hot water, added to the casein mixture and diluted with 12 litres of water.

Clear casein paint coat

If a wipe-resistant finish with the natural colour of the clay render is desired, the required paint coat has to be clear. This can be achieved with a mixture consisting of 1 part non-fat curd and 1.8 to 2 parts water, which is then supplemented by 1/8 to 1/9 part of lime powder. Due to a fine crystallic structure, this mixture creates a clear to slightly milky satin finish.

Further lime washes with stabilising Additives

According to historic sources, mixing lime with liquid manure instead of whey will also lead to a resistant finish. Urea and ammonium acetate increase the strength of china clay. This ancient knowledge was already used by the Chinese thousands of years ago: they produced extremely thin china with a clay mixture containing decomposing urine. A tested and tried version recommends the use of 70 g of animal (bone) glue, which is diluted in half a litre of boiling water and then mixed with 1 kg of lime. The following additives increase abrasion factor, wipe and weather resistance of lime whitewashes:

– Rye flour paste made of 1 part rye flour

boiled with 15 parts water and some zinc sulfate
– Agave juice
– Juice of boiled banana leaves
– Juice of prickly pear cactus (opuntia)
– Juice of the candelabra plant (euphorbia lacteal)
– Kapok seed oil
– Linseed oil, linseed oil varnish

Paint coats of non-washable distemper and whitening

Non-washable distemper and whitening paints are only suitable for interior finishes and are not wipe-resistant. For non-washable distemper, a primer coat is required.

Silicate paints and others commercial paints

Of course, all commercially available, industrial paints can be used as a coating. However, it is important to ensure that the exterior paint has a low vapour-retarding effect, which is usually the case with silicate paints. However, many manufacturers do not indicate the diffusion capacity of the paints on the paint bucket.

Water-repellent treatment

Interior plaster in wet rooms or exterior earth render that is supposed to be water-repellent and possess a natural appearance should receive a water-repellent treatment. Due to water-repellent treatments, the moisturising angle of the water drops with respect to the impregnated surface is higher than 90 degrees (12.11). The hydrophobic substance seeps into the pores of the material without sealing them; in other words, it reduces capillary absorbency of the material without dramatically obstructing vapour diffusion. Hydrophobic substances are usually diluted in organic alcohols, hydrocarbons or water. In the following a few substances that are used as water-repellent treatment:
– Silane or siloxane
– Polysiloxane (silicon resin)
– Siliconate

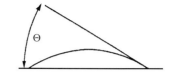

$\Theta \to 0 \quad \cos \Theta \to 1$

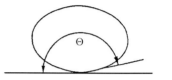

$90° < \Theta < 180° \to \quad \cos \Theta = -\sin(\Theta\text{-}90°)$

12.11

– Acrylic resin
– Silicic acid ester with water-repellent additives
– Silicates with water-repellent additives

Silane, siloxane and silicon resin chemically react with mineral building materials and are extremely weather-resistant. They reduce water absorption by more than 90 %, but vapour diffusion only by 5 to 8 %. Acrylic resin and silicic acid ester provide a comparable water resistance, but they also further reduce vapour diffusion (12.13). Due to the varying ingredients of the common brands and since different kinds of earth plaster react differently to each product, water-repellent treatments should be tested on a sample patch. The water absorption coefficients (w-values) of the earth-plastered, twice water-repellent treated samples tested at the Research Laboratory for Experimental Building (FEB) at the University of Kassel (12.12) range between 0.0 and 0.2 kg/m²h$^{0.5}$. The water absorption coefficient w denotes the amount of water that is absorbed by a unit area of building material within a specific time (Minke 2001). In a so-called flooding procedure, two wet coats of water-repellent treatment are applied in quick succession by means of a roller that is moved downwards along the surface creating a continuous repellent film. The treated surface must be dry and have a temperature not below 8 °C and not above 25 °C. When silane or siloxane is used, the surface should be moist, but not wet. The guidelines of use of the manufacturer have to be observed. After one or more years, the coats can be renewed. The very thin hydrophobic layers are susceptible to mechanical damage. They are often locally damaged by small scratches and then allow water to penetrate. Visible damage to the surface can be the consequence.

Weatherboarding

For the protection of straw bale walls, rear-ventilated timber boarding is an effective and simple solution (12.25). However, this solution also requires the straw bales to be plastered – ideally with a sprayed-on earth plaster – to comply with fire pro-

tection requirements, to prevent nesting of insects and vermin and to increase wind-tightness. The types of cladding most suitable for this kind of use are conventional or vertical weatherboarding or a cladding of watertight plywood panels or engineered wood products. All boarding requires substructures.

It is advantageous if the supporting structure for non-loadbearing straw bale constructions can simultaneously serve as the substructure for the boarding. For the Austrian research project S-House (Wimmer/ Drack/Hohensinner 2006) a straw screw was developed, which enables the façade substructure to be connected directly to the straw bales (12.14, see also p. 128).

Type of paint coat	Coating thickness g/m²	W-value kg/m²·h^{0,5}	Remarks
Without coating	0	9,5	
Linseed oil varnish	400	0,0	
Lime-casein mixture 1:1	420/350	0,6/1.5	0-6h/6-24h
Lime-casein mixture 1:8	'300/300	0,7	
Siline ink (van Baerle)	700/250/310	0,3	+ fixative
Hydrophob (Herbol)	390/390	0,0	
Baysilone LD (Bayer)	400/290	0,2	
Sylrit (Metroark)	350/320	0,0	
BS15 (Wacker)	450/430	0,1	
Stone hardener H (Wacker)	290/290	0,0	

12.12

TREEPLAST-Strohschraube
Länge 365 mm, ø 37 mm

12.14

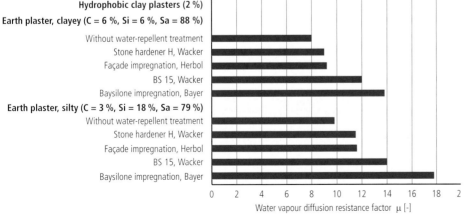

12.13

12.11 Water drop on a non-water-repellent treated surface (top) and on a water-repellent treated surface (bottom)

12.12 Water absorption coefficients (w-values) of earth plasters with various coatings

12.13 Increase of the water vapour diffusion resistance of earth plasters (C = clay, Si = silt, Sa = sand)

12.14 Treeplast straw screw made from biopolymer plastic and developed for the S-House in Böheimkirchen

13   Building costs, self-building and construction times

Building costs

There is no clear-cut answer to whether a straw bale building is less expensive than a conventional building. What kind of building should a straw bale house be compared to and which kind of wall construction can serve as a reference? As a general rule, any comparison should presuppose the same thermal insulation value of the walls. In such cases, a loadbearing straw bale wall construction is certainly less expensive in terms of material costs.

In the case of non-loadbearing straw bale walls, the cost depends on the type and position of the loadbearing timber structure. A major cost factor is the time-required to render the bales *(13.1)*. Facing plaster or render surfaces require at least three coats on each side of the bales, including prior filling of gaps and holes and levelling of the surface – all of which is considerably more time-consuming and costly than masonry construction.

A more time and cost-saving option is to line the inner face with gypsum fibreboard or plasterboard, or another wood-composite panel, but this comes at the cost of less thermal storage mass in the interior.

A further factor in the evaluation of financial viability is whether work undertaken by the client, family and friends (self-building) can be factored out of cost calculations. In the case of a timber frame construction with straw infill, earth plaster on the interior and lime render or boarding on the exterior, a

significant proportion of the work can be undertaken by laypeople, which can contribute to reducing the overall building costs. The cost of straw bales is substantially lower than that of conventional insulation materials, but they represent only a small fraction of the total costs.

A study in Austria compared the costs of insulation materials with the same thermal insulation effect. Not counting the cost of delivery to the building site, a 30-cm-thick layer of straw costs 3.65€ per m² of wall surface. Cellulose fibre insulation costs five times that, and 24-cm-thick rock wool insulation 6.5 times. At a uniform installation cost of 22 €/m², the total cost of a 150 m² house made with straw bales was 2.6 % less than the same house insulated with cellulose insulation and 3.6 % less than one insulated with rock wool insulation (GrAT 2001). It is, however, unrealistic to assume the same installation costs for all three variants.

Figure *13.1* shows the production costs of a wall with a timber frame structure and straw bale infill for a single-family house in Hamburg designed by Dirk Scharmer and completed in 2012. Of the total costs, 28 % are for the timber construction, 16 % for the straw bales and 48 % for the three-layer plaster coat inside and outside.

Self-building

The installation of straw bales as thermal insulation for wall, roof and floor constructions are all tasks that can be undertaken by the aspiring self-builder. Similarly, the finishing of wall surfaces including plugging gaps, trimming smooth the surface and plastering or lining wall surfaces with boarding are suitable self-building tasks. The preparation and application of earth plaster, however, can be extremely labour-intensive without professional equipment and it may be worth considering leaving this to suitably equipped experienced contractors. Cladding walls and treating plaster surfaces or coating with paints, varnishes or the like are likewise activities that can easily be undertaken by the self-building client and can bring substantial cost savings.

Clients should think carefully about what construction tasks they feel they could undertake themselves at an early stage in the project planning. In most cases, people overestimate their own abilities and avail-able time and at the same time underestimate the work involved. This can lead to time and financial bottlenecks as well as social tensions. It is, therefore, important to realistically and systematically assess one's own capabilities and capacities.

Construction times

In a project in Kaliningrad, a house for orphans designed by Minke et al. and built chiefly with laypeople, the construction times were documented. It is interesting to note that erecting the straw bale walls accounted for only 18 % of the work but that smoothing and finishing the surfaces required 20 % of the working time. This was certainly due in part to the fact that plaster was applied directly to the straw bales (without a plaster base) and therefore all gaps had been conscientiously plugged and the surfaces trimmed flat with hedge trimmers. The use of a plaster base would have reduced the amount of work needed to plug gaps and create a smooth surface with the hedge trimmers. Even so, plastering the walls still took at least twice as long as constructing the walls of straw bales.

The total workload amounted to 6.6 hours per m² of wall surface, which is on the high side. One reason for this was that the time required for the production and transport of the earth plaster (26 %) and the manual application of the second and third coats of plaster (20 %) was so high because a suitable compulsory mixer was not available to mix the clay and the plastering work was carried out by laypeople with virtually no prior experience of plastering. In addition, the sub-optimal mixing of the plaster resulted in sometimes significant shrinkage cracks after drying that needed subsequent repairing.

Quantity	Position	Unit price	Total price	€/m²	Proportion
0.84 m³	Delivery of timber	450.00 €/m³	377.91 €	23.75 €/m²	9 %
3.12 m	Install sole plate	11.00 €/m	34.32 €	2.16 €/m²	1 %
15.91 m²	Construct and rect timber frame	29.00 €/m²	461.45 €	29.00 €/m²	11 %
7.00 m	Prepare and install bracing	47.00 €/m	329.00 €	20.68 €/m²	8 %
	Timber, supply and construction			**75.58 €/m²**	**28 %**
5.73 m³	Delivery of straw bales	48.00 €/m³	274.96 €	17.28 €/m²	6 %
15.91 m²	Install straw bales	26.00 €/m²	413.71 €	26.00 €/m²	10 %
	Plaster base on wood, inside and outside			**43.28 €/m²**	**16 %**
77.76 m	Plaster base on wood, inside and outside	3.00 €/m	233.28 €	14.66 €/m²	5 %
15.91 m²	Clay plaster, inside, undercoat	15.00 €/m²	238.68 €	15.00 €/m²	6 %
15.91 m²	Clay plaster, inside, 2nd + 3rd coat	30.00 €/m²	477.36 €	30.00 €/m²	11 %
15.91 m²	Plaster reinforcement, inside	5.00 €/m²	79.56 €	5.00 €/m²	2 %
	Wall surface, inside			**64.66 €/m²**	**24 %**
15.91 m²	Clay render, outside, undercoat	20.00 €/m²	318.24 €	20.00 €/m²	7 %
15.91 m²	Clay render, outside, 2nd + 3rd coat	39.00 €/m²	620.57 €	39.00 €/m²	15 %
15.91 m²	Plaster reinforcement, outside	5.00 €/m²	79.56 €	5.00 €/m²	2 %
	Wall surface, outside			**64.00 €/m²**	**24 %**
15.91 m²	Coating. outside. vapour permeable. hydrophobic	12.00 €/m²	190.94 €	12.00 €/m²	4 %
15.91 m²	Chalk-casein coating	8.00 €/m²	127.30 €	8.00 €/m²	3 %
	Coatings, supply and application			**20.00 €/m²**	**7 %**
	Net total		4256.84€	267.52 €/m²	100 %

13 .1

13.1 Costs of a straw bale wall (timber frame construction with straw bale infill) based on the example of a single-family house near Hamburg. Prices as of 2012

Had a ready-mix mortar been used and pre-pared with a suitable compulsory mixer, the construction time per square metre could have been reduced by 1.5 to 2.5 h/m². Overall, the total amount of work and therefore time required to produce a straw bale wall, including plastering on both sides, is considerably higher than the time required for a corresponding masonry wall made of large-format lightweight perfo-rated bricks or aerated concrete blocks. As a rule, straw bale construction is therefore only more economical when the client un-dertakes part of the work themselves.

Planning permission

In many countries, not only timber con-structions with straw bale insulation but also loadbearing straw bale structures are officially permitted. Various states in the USA have passed specific regulations for straw bale building stipulating the maxi-mum moisture content of the bales, mini-mum wall thickness, maximum loading of the walls and corresponding finishing treat-ments. The most detailed regulations are given in the California Straw Bale Building Code (see King 2006), and in the Arizona Straw Bale Building Code (see Magwood/ Mack 2002, p. 219). In France, official rules for straw bale building were issued in 2012 by the Réseau Français de la Construction en Paille: *Règles professionnelles de la construction en paille*. The European Tech-nical Assessment ETA-17/0247, issued on 17 June 2017, also provides guidance on obtaining a permit for straw bale buildings. In Denmark, France, Great Britain, the Netherlands, Ireland and Switzerland, plan-ning permission has also been granted for straw bale buildings.
In Ship Harbour in Nova Scotia, Cana-da, planning permission was given for a two-storey house with loadbearing straw bale walls (Magwood/Mack 2002, p. 199). Another two-storey building with loadbearing straw bale walls was permitted and built in 2002 in Disentis, Switzerland,

and even a three-storey house in South Tyrol *(see p. 122)*. In Germany, specific planning approval (ZiE) has now been given for many loadbearing buildings.

Building permits in Germany

In Germany, only regulated building prod-ucts, i.e. those with appropriate technical approval, may be used for construction. These are listed in the Construction Prod-ucts Lists Parts A and B (Bauregellisten) issued by the DIBt in Berlin, the official technical authority for building products and techniques.
Non-regulated construction products may be used if the construction product has either
1. General Building Inspectorate Type Approval (AbZ),
2. General Building Inspectorate Test Certificate (AbP), or
3. Specific planning approval (ZiE – Zu-lassung im Einzelfall) for the respective individual case.

Building products that exhibit normal or lower flammability, that are not subject to further fire, sound or thermal insulation requirements, and which serve no structural function (see Construction Products List Part C) are exempt from these requirements. Since external walls made of straw bales generally act as thermal insulation, the exemption does not apply in such cases, but it can apply to non-loadbearing internal walls made of straw bales.
As mentioned earlier, General Building Inspectorate Type Approval (AbZ) is now available for "straw bales for construction" that permits their use for a limited range of applications. The document is available from the German Straw Bale Construction Association (FASBA e.V., www.fasba.de). Straw bales for use in accordance with the approval must possess a certificate of conformity (Ü-symbol).
For building products "…whose use does not serve to fulfil significant requirements

for the safety of building structures […], a general test certificate (AbP) issued by the building inspectorate may suffice in place of a general type approval (AbZ)…" (see §19 MBO – National model building code, also e.g. §18 HBO – Federal building code for the state of Hesse). A General Building Inspectorate Test Certificate (AbP) is likewise available for straw bales. In conjunction with Construction Products List Part C No. 1.3, straw bales may be used for "external wall infill […] with a post spacing of ≤ 1.0 m if they do not serve to ensure the stability of a building or its parts." As with the AbZ, when using straw bales in accordance with the AbP, straw bale producers are required to provide a corresponding certificate of conformity (Ü-symbol).
If straw bales are to be used outside the provisions of the AbZ or AbP, specific planning approval (ZiE) is required for each individual case from the respective federal building authority. Many of the federal building authorities in the different federal states of Germany have granted such approval for straw bale buildings and are generally cooperative. In the federal states of Rhineland-Palatinate, Bavaria and Hesse, approval has even been granted for load-bearing straw bale buildings made of large bales, in Mecklenburg-Western Pomerania for loadbearing barrel vaults made of small bales *(see p. 138)* and in Lower Saxony for a five-storey building made of timber elements insulated with straw bales *(see p. 132)*.

14 The building process

14.1

14.2

Prior to installation, all bales have to be assessed in regard to their quality *(see chapter 3, p. 22)*.

Straw bales and in particular loose straw present an increased fire hazard during the construction phase. Therefore the construction site must be kept clean at all times. Straw bale walls should receive a first plaster layer right after completion *(see chapter 4, p. 32)*.

Transport and storage

Arms, legs and hands should be protected with appropriate working gear when handling straw bales. Also, a breathing mask should be worn. Straw bales should be stored on pallets or planks or on a completely dry floor and have to be protected from rain. Bales with a moisture content of more than 15 % are not suitable for construction. Moist bales should be exposed to the wind and stored in rows to dry. It is advisable to store bales in separate marked stacks according to their length: as building practice has shown, it is very timeconsuming to find and repeatedly measure bales of a certain length when they are needed.

Supplementary compaction of the bales

If the straw bales are not sufficiently compressed, that is if their density in dry condition is less than at least 90 kg/m³, supplementary compaction becomes necessary. This can be conducted in a very simple way as shown in figure *14.1:* under imposed

weight the strings can be shortened with a toggle that can be pushed into the bale. At the Research Laboratory for Experimental Building (FEB) at the University of Kassel, a bale press was built with a car jack so that the bales could be lifted and compacted *(14.2)*.

Separating of bales

Often, not the full length of a bale is required but only a part to suit corners, doors or windows. In such an event, bales can be separated and newly tied up with the help of straw bale needles as shown in figure *14.3*. Needles with handle, tip and eye can be simply manufactured from 6-mm structural steel. The ends of the steel profile can be forged with a hammer into a handle and a flattened tip, which is then sharpened. Into this end the "eye" of the needle of about 4 mm diameter can be drilled and edges should be deburred. The needles are used to replace the bales' original strings: two equal ends of new string are threaded through the eye of the needle and poked through the bale perpendicular to the original strings *(14.4, 14.5)*. The new string is then cut – with the needle pulled back out – and both ends are tied. This procedure is repeated for the second original string. After this, the old bale strings can be cut and the bale separated in two parts. The needle should penetrate the bale at the joint between two flakes to enable clean separation of the halves. As shown in figure *14.3*, a double-needle can be

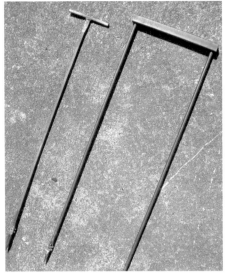

14.3

14.6

14.8

14.4

14.9

14.5

14.1 Simple additional compaction of straw bales

14.2 Gadget for additional compaction of straw bales, developed by the Research Laboratory for Experimental Building (FEB)

14.3 Needles for the separation of bales

14.4 Pushing the needles into the bale

14.5 Threading of new strings

14.6 Creating notches in the bales

14.7 Reshaping of bales

14.8 Wooden sticks are driven through the straw bales

14.9 Movable connection between straw bale and timber post

14.10 Laterally reinforcing the wall with bamboo or timber laths

14.11, 14.12 Prestressing of wall by tensioned straps

used to facilitate the entire procedure; the distance between the needles is the same as between the strings.

Reshaping of bales

Notches in the bales for columns can be easily manufactured with a chain saw (14.6). However, care should be taken not to cut the strings of the bales. Bales can be reshaped to suit curved walls. This can be done by bending as shown in figure 14.7.

Bale installation

Before the installation of rear-ventilated façade systems, an insect mesh must be fitted. For loadbearing straw bale walls the position of windows and doors should be marked beforehand, and upright planks should be placed at the corners for support and to check perpendicular wall installation. Usually, bales are laid horizontally in a running bond except if they are stacked snug between framing posts. Reinforcing steel rods in the bottom wall layers – as are common in the USA – are not required if the wall is prestressed or stabilised by a post-and-beam structure. These rods can even be a liability as they are thermally coupled to the foundation and may assist condensation within the bales, which may lead to damages.

Wall reinforcement

Loadbearing or free-standing straw bale walls can be reinforced with sharpened bamboo or wooden sticks, which are driven into the bales vertically or at an angle. They should be at least 2.5 cm thick and should penetrate approx. two and a half bale courses (14.8). If the straw bales are stacked in front of or behind the timber posts, they should be fixed back to them every other course. Figure 14.9 shows such a connection that is movable. When pre-tensioning the wall, i.e. pressing down the bales, it can slide down along the supports. In this case. the fastener is connected to a ladder-shaped horizontal bracing element. Thin vertical bamboo or timber laths that are positioned in pairs on either side of the wall and connected to each other during the stacking process provide a reinforcing solution (14.10). Plastering, however, is more work as a plaster base has to be used.

Wall prestressing

Loadbearing straw bale walls need to be prestressed before loads can be imposed. However, prestressing is also advisable for non-loadbearing systems. To achieve pre-compression for loadbearing structures, a ring beam on top of the walls is required, which is then connected to the foundation with tension ties – for example threaded rods. If tensioned rods are used, they have

to be threaded in through the bales, which is time-consuming and requires the rods to be segmented. A simpler method involves tensioned straps, which are fixed to the foundation and tied around the top ring beam (14.11, 14.12) or which are even running below the base slab. Occasionally, the straps may obstruct the rendering of the wall. Additional prestressing might be unnecessary altogether if the roof imposes sufficient load onto the walls. In the case of non-loadbearing systems, it may be useful to assign a double function to inferior purlins: roof support as well as ring beam for the walls. The threaded rods and tension ties need to be spaced depending on the required tension, the bending strength of the ring beam and the type of stretching device used – general rules do not apply. In any event, major deformation of the ring beam must be prevented. The bales of non-loadbearing walls should be stacked starting from the first layer to the one before last and then strapped tight. Finally, the last bale course can be introduced below the inferior purlin/ring beam (14.13) and the straps removed. For this prestressing hydraulic or pneumatic jacks can be used as well (14.14, 14.15), provided that a stable roof construction exists which can support the jacks. The hydraulic jack in figure 14.14 can exert up to 3 tonnes of pressure. It is normally used for trucks and

14.10

14.11

14.12

14.13

14.14

buses. Loadbearing straw bale walls can also be prestressed with timber profiles. The profiles are screwed onto the ring beam on top and fixed to the foundation via steel angles with elongated holes. The bales have to be compressed with straps beforehand to ensure that the timber profiles will retain their tension. The timber profiles also provide a good substructure for exterior boarding and interior plaster base.

Retensioning of loadbearing walls

The relaxation *(see chapter 6, p. 39)* causes the applied preload to partially relax over time. If the preload falls below the tension generated by the roof load, the wall begins to shrink. To prevent this from happening, sufficiently high stresses have to be applied. This can hardly be done on the construction site. A promising method frequently used in practice is retensioning. This is done by increasing the prestressing load over a specific period of time repeatedly. At present there are no scientific studies on the effect of retensioning. A sufficient pretensioning is achieved when walls from flat bales are compressed by 14 % and walls from upright bales by 10 %. The following prodecure for retensioning can be followed: Retensioning happens one hour after the first prestressing, then again two, four, 16, 32 hours after the previous retensioning; thereafter every 72 hours. Before and after retension-

ing, the wall has to be measured precisely. The retensioning works must be continued at least for three weeks. After that the post-tensioning work can be completed provided that no more height changes in the wall occurred (Krick 2008).

Removal of deformations

After installation, free-standing or load-bearing straw bale walls may show signs of locally restricted deformation. On most occasions, these can be removed with a mallet or a self-made beater *(14.17, 14.18)*.

Back-filling of joints and gaps

Before rendering a straw bale wall, the bales must be smoothed and all cavities and gaps are filled beforehand with loose straw soaked in light clay sludges. The same material can be used to level slight dents *(14.19)*.

Cropping of bale surfaces

Before rendering a straw bale wall, it may be useful to crop back protruding stalks with a hedge trimmer *(14.20, 14.21)*.

Rendering of the walls

If the wall is to be earth-rendered, a runny undercoat with high clay content should be applied first. This layer should be applied with high pressure and is best sprayed on with a pump. The render should be rather fluid to penetrate at least 1 cm below the

surface immersing all stalks. Stalk ends are smoothed over with a board or a trowel. For more details, see *chapter 12, p. 64*.

French-dip technique

With this technique, developed by the French builder Tom Rijven, the straw bale will be immersed completely for a few seconds into a liquid clay slurry so that the clay penetrates 3–5 cm into the bale and all outside straw stalks are covered with a thin layer of earth plaster. After the dipping, the excess sludge has to be brushed off with a board and the bales can be placed on pallets, for example, for drying. The advantage of this technique lies in the fact that the earth plaster that will be applied later adheres very well to the bale and that the straw bale wall does not require trimming. The disadvantage of this technology is that the drying process requires rain-protected storage area; also, the bales have a much higher weight and a long drying time is needed (Rijven 2008).

Trial and error – an example

The test building described in the next few paragraphs highlights graphically the many mistakes that can be committed during the planning and construction stages of a straw bale building, the problems that they may cause and how those problems can be solved. The building was conceived and

14.15

14.16

14.17

14.18

erected by 12 students during the summer of 2000 as part of the "Building with straw bales" workshop at the University of Kassel guided by Gernot Minke and Dittmar Hecken. In summer 2001, another group of students guided by Gernot Minke and Friedemann Mahlke removed damages and completed the building. The structure was to accommodate a 36-m² multi-purpose room for seminars at minimal cost, using a simple construction that lends itself to do-it-yourself building and the use of environment-friendly building materials. Loads from the green roof with a 15-cm soil layer and planted with wild weeds and herbs were to be supported only by the walls *(14.21)*. Loadbearing straw bale walls require roof loads to be evenly distributed, effectively resulting in a regular geometrical plan – in this case a square was chosen *(14.19)*. The roof structure consists of round timber profiles (tree trunks) and carries a central skylight that allows even daylighting into the space. Three additional full-height windows and a door at the corner provide additional lighting. Instead of four strip foundations, eight point or elephant's feet foundations with concrete beams supporting the walls were constructed to save labour and cost *(14.20)*. The beams supporting the walls are continuous beams with equal bending moments in the middle and at the ends, which leads only to minimal deflection. A ring beam consisting of half a 24 to 28-cm

round timber pole is riding on top of the walls. Perpendicular boards were nailed to the beam to increase the supporting surface area and structural interaction with the bales *(14.22)*. An extremely simple low-cost solution was found for the floor build-up: the ground was refilled with a 10-cm layer of crushed rock and compacted with a tamper. This was covered with a 3-cm layer of sand *(14.24)* followed by PE foil as horizontal moisture barrier *(14.25)*. Recycled timber pallets serve as ventilated substructure for the straw bales; floating 24-mm OSB boards were laid – without additional battens – directly onto the bales, and the joints were sealed with 25-mm-wide screwed-on OSB strips.

Construction – the first attempt
Construction proceeded as follows: first of all, the base beams carrying the walls were positioned on the foundations and the gaps closed with boards to prevent mice and insects from nesting there *(14.23)*. Next, the windows and the door frames were erected at the corners and fixed to the bottom beams with diagonal braces *(14.24)*. For everyone the most satisfactory part of the building process was the installation of the bales *(14.8)*: the walls took shape very quickly and were completed after only one and a half day. Since the bales exercised considerable pressure onto the window frames, they had to be connected with

14.13 Installation of the last bale course

14.14 Hydraulic jack

14.15 Pneumatic jack

14.16 Deformations in the wall can be corrected with a mallet

14.17 Gaps filled with loose straw soaked in clay sludge

14.18 Cropping of the bale surface with hedge trimmer

tensioned straps (14.28) and the window embrasures were reinforced with screwed-on timber battens. The straw bales were reinforced with sharpened wooden sticks, which were driven diagonally into the bales, penetrating approx. two and a half bale courses (14.8). The roof consists of rafters, each supported by the adjacent rafter, and nailed timber boarding with a 2-mm fibrous polyester matting for mechanical protection of the roofing membrane (14.26, 14.27). This is made of PVC-coated polyester fabric whose individual courses were welded together to form a continuous membrane. Sleepers were mounted onto the roof to withstand shear forces of the green roof layer (14.28). The roof parapet is formed by a round timber profile which accepts the resulting shear forces from the sleepers and the substrate and is fixed to the rafters via spacers. To accommodate the expected strong compression of the bales, a roof deflection of 25 cm had been allowed for from the beginning. After applying the full load, the roof actually did reach this deflection within several hours. However, unexpectedly the walls buckled to such a degree that collapse of the building seemed immanent and the roof had to be propped up. The main reason for this failure was the physical constitution of the bales: they were very fresh and were far too moist, they had not been sufficiently compressed. Subsequent measurements showed that the density was only 60–70 kg/m3. There were two further structural reasons for the failure: the door opening was wider than the windows. Thus, the bales adjacent to the door received higher loads from the roof than the other bales. Here, deformation was also most severe. A fourth reason is arguably the great slenderness of the seven-bale-high wall, which increases the risk for deformation.

Solving the problems – the second attempt
Once the errors had been recognised, the roof was temporarily propped up and then slowly lifted with car jacks by about 20 cm so that the straw bales could be easily

removed. The bales were then compacted with a self-made bale press and newly tied up (14.2). Hence, the required density of 80–90 kg/m3 could be achieved. Finally, the compacted bales could be re-installed. Additional timber planks of 4/30 cm were positioned on top of the third and sixth course of bales and in between the window embrasures to improve stability. The boards form a sort of tongue-and-groove connection with the screwed-on timber battens of the embrasures preventing horizontal but allowing vertical movement. Additional thin bamboo sticks were spaced at 40 cm and driven into the bales below the planks to increase friction between planks and bales (14.29). After installation of the seventh – final – course, bales were strapped down to achieve maximum prestressing/ compression. As it turned out, broad straps with a maximum tensile strength of 1000 kg were required. Thinner straps simply were not suitable to achieve the required pressure. As an alternative method, a heavy truck jack was "wedged" between roof structure and the seventh bale course to compact the bales (14.14). The achieved state of compression could then even be secured with thinner straps. Now, the last course of bales could be slid in and the straps removed. The scaffolding poles were gradually winded down until full bearing on the walls had been reestablished. This way, buckling of the wall could securely be prevented. Creeping of the bales as a result of the roof loads subsided after a few weeks and – after a quick makeover with the hedge trimmer – the walls could be plastered. The undercoat was sprayed on with a selfmade rendering pump. Clay slurry was pressurised in a tank and sprayed onto the walls with a hose. Pressure was kept constant at approx. 5 bar by means of a small compressor. After spraying, the walls were smoothed with the hands or with a trowel until all stalks were immersed and levelled.

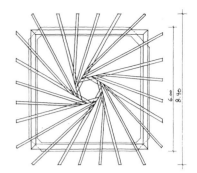

14.19

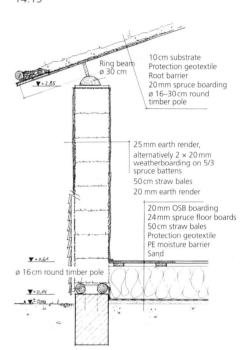

14.20

14.21

14.22

14.23

14.24

14.26

14.27

14.25

14.28

14.29

14.19 Roof plan showing rafters

14.20 Wall section

14.21 The completed structure with its green roof

14.22 A timber pole cut in half serves as the ringbeam.

14.23 Base beams were closed off against mice with boards.

14.24 Connection of timber frame with bottom beams

14.25 PE foil was used in the floor construction as moisture barrier.

14.26 Rafters make up the roof.

14.27 Nailed timber boarding cover the roof rafters.

14.28 The bales were connected with tensioned straps.

14.29 Bamboo sticks were driven into the bales.

II Built examples in detail

Single-family home
Bryson City, North Carolina, USA

Design: Sustainable Structures
Straw bale works: Bill Green
Wall system: Timber frame with straw infill
Completion: 2001
Floor area: approx. 220 m²

The small town of Bryson City at the edge of the Great Smoky Mountains National Park in North Carolina was an ideal place for building with and within nature. The completed three-storey straw bale building nestles neatly into the mountainous environment and is ideal for various outdoor activities of the clients and the travel business they operate.

The building comprises non-loadbearing straw bale walls with primary timber structure. As is still the custom in the US, chicken wire was introduced into the render of the straw bales, which is believed to increase the strength of the render. But rather the contrary is the case: the wire obstructs movements of the structure, thus assisting the formation of cracks and fissures.

1

2

1 The house under construction
2 Living area with earth render
3 Bedroom with exposed timber lintel
4 Exterior view of residence with carport

3

4

Single-family home
Lower Lake, California, USA

Design: Pete Gang and Kelly Lerner,
One World Design
Site supervision: Client
Wall system: Rice straw insulated and
plastered timber structure
Completion: 2001
Floor area: approx. 148 m²

This house for a non-medical practitioner
in Northern California is largely a do-it-
yourself construction. After being designed
by the architects, it was built with the help
of friends, acquaintances and a few hired
hands within one year. It nestles into a
5-hectare site covered with oak trees and is
the first earth-rendered straw bale building
that received planning permission in California. The client – a female artist working
with ceramics – seized the opportunity
to design every single room individually,
using paint coats with natural pigments in
addition to the earth and lime render. The
house is orientated according to passive
solar principles and possesses highly efficient cellulose insulation; thus, hardly any
additional heating is required. A cooling
tower and large roof overhangs (shading)
keep the building cool during summer;
under-floor heating and a little stove can
bridge supply shortfalls during winter.
Connection to the public supply grid was
not necessary since hot water and electrici-
ty are produced with solar energy.

1

1 Bedroom
2 Garden view with cooling tower
3 Large roof overhands provide shade
4 Exterior view with trellis

2

3

4

Single-family home
Lake Biwa, Japan

Design: Goichi Oiwa (Seian University of Art and Design)
Wall system: Timber structure with rice straw bale insulation, reed insulation on top floor
Completion: 2003
Floor area: 140 m²

The house situated at Lake Biwa, Japan's largest lake, is one of the first buildings in Japan that use rice straw for the insulation of walls.
Straw bales were used for the walls on the ground floor while reed was used for the upper floor and the roof; the latter was clad with derived timber boards.
The straw bales were rendered, employing various traditional techniques: for the exterior render Tosasshikkui was used. This is a lime-earth finish with added straw, which is supposed to minimise cracking. In the entrance hall, Kakiotoshi was chosen – an earth-straw mix that was keyed with a steel brush and results in a rustic Japanese interior. In the kitchen, the slightly shimmering earth finish – Otsumigaki – was achieved by polishing the still wet render with a smooth trowel or stones.

1

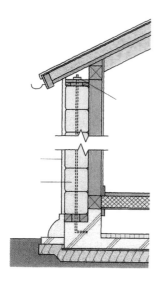

2

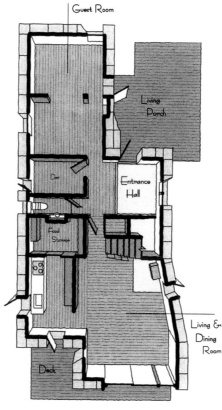

3

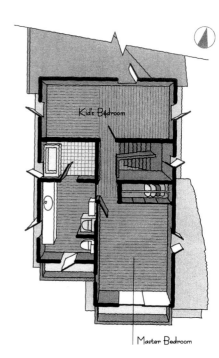

4

5

6

7

1 Reed was used as roof insulation

2 Wall section

3 Ground floor plan

4 First floor plan

5 Exterior view with garden deck

6 Reed infill in the walls of the upper floor

7 Exterior view with front porch

Christie Walk
Adelaide, Australia

Design: Paul Downton
Wall system: Timber post-and-beam structure with straw bale infill
Completion: 2006
Floor areas: 125 m² (SB 1), 75 m² (SB 2), 114 m² (SB 3), 114 m² (SB 4)

Christie Walk is a community-initiated not-for-profit project that was intended to provide a working example of a "piece of ecocity". As well as its attention to a very strong environmental ethos, the provision of external space for gardens and community benefit sets this pioneering "ecocity" project apart from "business-as-usual" Australian development. It is an inner-city development funded by individuals in the wider community with no conventional developer and no government assistance; all borrowings were derived from ethical finance sources.

Christie Walk contains 27 dwellings in four buildings on an inner-city site of just 2000 m². All dwellings have double-glazing (which is still not mandatory in Australia!), all timber is recycled or plantation-sourced and insulation levels are high. There was considerably more green space created on site than existed before this redevelopment. Determination to provide only eleven car spaces on the site precipitated a big change in attitude towards inner-city car ownership by the city council.

The four straw bale houses of this project have a timber post-and-beam structure on concrete slabs with rendered non-loadbearing straw bale external walls.

1

1 Three-storey house SB 1 across community garden

2 Two-storey straw bale cottage SB 2 and roof garden on adjacent building

3 SB 2 under construction

4 Exterior view of two-storey straw bale cottage SB 2

5 Site plan

2

3

4

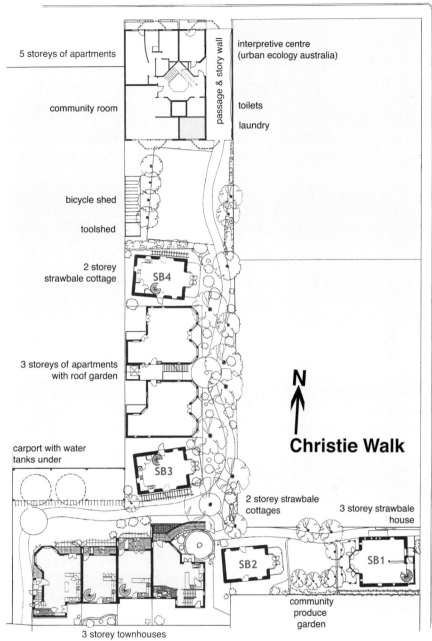

STURT STREET

5 storeys of apartments

community room

passage & story wall

interpretive centre
(urban ecology australia)

toilets

laundry

bicycle shed

toolshed

2 storey
strawbale cottage

SB4

3 storeys of apartments
with roof garden

carport with water
tanks under

SB3

N

Christie Walk

2 storey strawbale
cottages

3 storey strawbale
house

SB2

SB1

community
produce
garden

3 storey townhouses

5

RUSSELL STREET

6

7

Straw Bale House SB1

This three-storey house contains two bedrooms on the first floor and a study on the top floor which is set into the pyramidal roof space. Its tight urban location made conventional solar orientation impossible. Its main windows, balcony and patio doors face west across a small shared community garden. The vegetation that was planned for the garden and west façade provide protection from the late afternoon and evening sun. The east façade of the house is directly on the street, with the front door in an entry porch set at a right angle to the public footpath and the estate's pedestrian entry gate. The footpath adjoins the house immediately to the north. The cement render deliberately follows the uneven surface of the straw bales, which were not trimmed to a conventional smooth finish.

Straw Bale House SB2

This two-bedroom, two-storey house was one of the smallest built in South Australia for several decades. It was the first building constructed on the project site and was a "collective self-build" with assistance from a number of volunteers over a period of about ten months. Its main windows, balcony and patio doors face east across a small shared community garden. The skim on the concrete render was lime-based and successful but was not repeated for the other straw bale houses because it was deemed too labour-intensive.

Straw Bale House SB3

In plan, SB3 is the mirror twin of SB4 and the orientation is entirely to do with fitting the site conditions. The exterior of the straw bale walls is rendered with cement and internally the finish is a white-painted plaster skim on a cement render base.

Straw Bale House SB4

SB4 faces the community room, kitchen and laundry on the ground floor of the five-storey apartment building across a courtyard that works as both a community space with a shared workshop and bicycle parking, and also as a partial car park. The owners chose to finish the interior with an ochre-tinted cement render which adds further character to differentiate the ambience of this house from its SB3 "twin".

8

9

10

11

6 Street view of three-storey house SB 1

7 Garden path between SB 1 and SB 2

8 Exterior view of SB 2 with community garden

9 SB 3 between townhouse terrace and three-storey apartment building

10 Kitchen tiles in SB 2

11 Interior view of three-storey house SB 1

H & H Residence at Taos, New Mexico, USA

Design: EDGE Architects, Pamela Freund and Kenneth Anderson
Builder: The Salamander Company – Patrick O'Brien and Robert Ivy
Wall system: Timber post-and-beam structure with straw bale infill
Completion: 2007
Floor area: 240 m²

The entry courtyard and greenhouse on the south side of the house create ideal growing environments while providing relief from the aridity of the high desert climate and radiating heat. They shield the rest of the house and allow fresh air inside when outdoor temperatures are cool. Sitting by the kiva fireplace in the living room or out on the screened porch adjacent to the dining room, one relishes the view of Taos Mountain. The sizable kitchen features a large island with stools that enjoys a tall clerestory space which brings light into the centre of the great room. The breakfast nook offers a long view over the western mesa. A porch off of the master bedroom and another courtyard on the west side define relaxing spaces from which to delight in the sunset. The walls are built of a timber post-and-beam structure with straw bale infill.

1

2

3

4

5

6

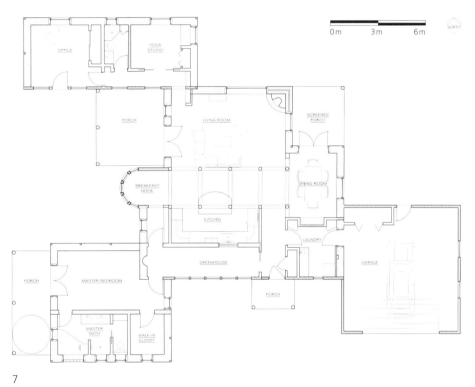

7

1 Exterior view

2 Porch outside the master bedroom

3 Interior wall with straw bale infill under construction

4 Interior view

5 Kitchen with clerestory above

6 Living room

7 Ground floor plan

Single-family home
Esslingen, Germany

Design: Erz und Gugel Architekten
Wall system: Prefabricated timber frame elements with straw bale infill
Completion: 2008
Floor area: 117 m²
Additional area: 53 m²
Construction costs: 1623 €/m²

The building planned as a passive house is located on a slope and was erected on a base of waterproof concrete. The storeys above are a timber frame structure built with I-joists. The joists were insulated with softwood fibreboards. The wall elements were prefabricated, insulated with vertical straw bales and then delivered to the site. In order to achieve the passive house standard with a U-value of 0.12 W/m²K, the structure was equipped with additional insulation made of softwood fibreboard. The airtight layer is achieved on the inside by glued OSB panels.
On the exterior, the building was given a larch wood cladding. A flat green roof is on top of the building. The house obtained a specific planning approval (ZiE) from the building authority.

1

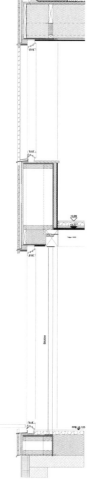
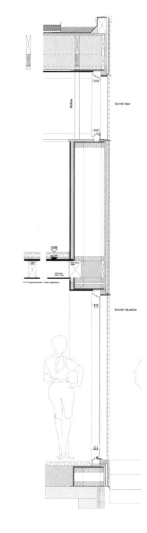

2

3

4

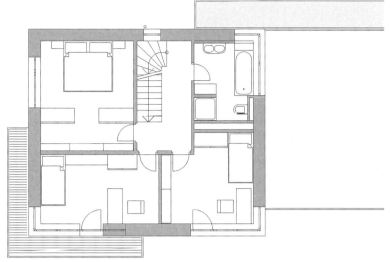

5

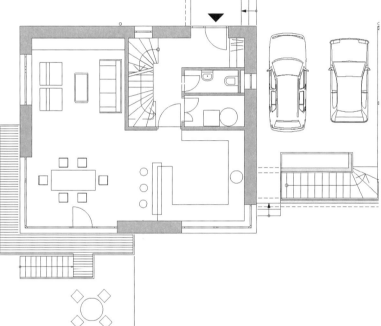

6

7

8

9

10

1 Exterior view

2 Wall sections

3 Exterior view

4 Interior

5 Roof plan

6 Ground floor plan

7 Corner with recessed window

8 Prefabrication of wall elements

9 Wall assembly by crane

10 Filling the timber structure with bales

Single-family home
Langenau, Germany

Design: Atelier Werner Schmidt
Wall system: Timber structure with straw
bale infill
Completion: 2009
Floor area: 125 m²

Floor, walls and roof of the house in Lan-
genau, near Ulm, have a 80-cm-thick straw
insulation. Both the base and the roof are
lined with jumbo bales, each measuring
120 × 80 × 240 cm. For the walls, smaller
Jumbo bales of 80 × 80 × 160 cm were
used. The roof structure rests on a solid
timber ceiling on which the bales were
placed. A green roof forms the upper cover.
The walls are plastered with clay on the
interior and with lime on the exterior. Only
initially does the roof construction appear
loadbearing: over time, the weight of the
roof compresses the straw bales, causing
the roof to lower slightly until the existing
timber structure bears the loads.

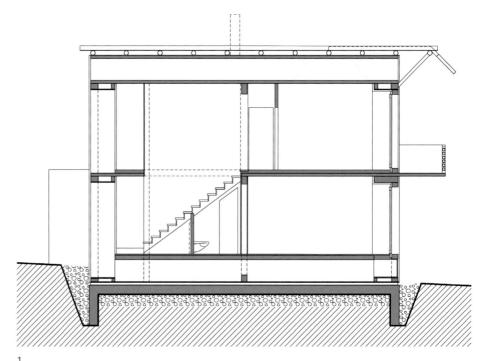

1

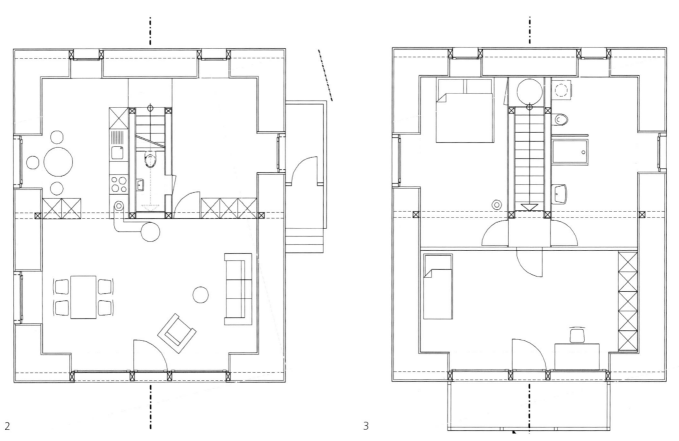

2   3

4

5

50

6

1 Section

2 Ground floor plan

3 First floor plan

4, 5 The house under construction: installation of timber frames for the windows, straw bales are inserted into the wall construction, installation of windows

6 Street façade with balcony

7 Garden façade

7

Vine Hill Residence
Sonoma County, California, USA

Design: Arkin Tilt Architects – Anni Tilt, David Arkin, Chandra Baerg
Wall system: I-joist timber frame with straw bale infill
Completion: 2011
Floor area: 208 m²

The home and caretaker unit are the centrepieces of a rural retreat located on 6 hectares in western Sonoma County, California. The site was a former Christmas tree farm with overgrown non-native conifers, cleared to reveal majestic oaks and redwoods, and the buildings were carefully sited to preserve and appreciate them. The three wings of the project – guest bedroom and studio, main living/dining/kitchen space and master bedroom suite – each enjoy a passive solar orientation. Together they surround a courtyard that extends the home's 208 m² of living space to the outdoors. The home stays comfortable through hot summer days without any mechanical air conditioning.
All walls are built of an I-joist timber frame with straw bale infill and finished with a lime plaster on both exterior and interior surfaces.

1

2

3

4

5

1 Dining/kitchen space with clerestory

2 The building under construction

3, 4 Entrance with trellis

5 Views of courtyard

6 Exterior view

6

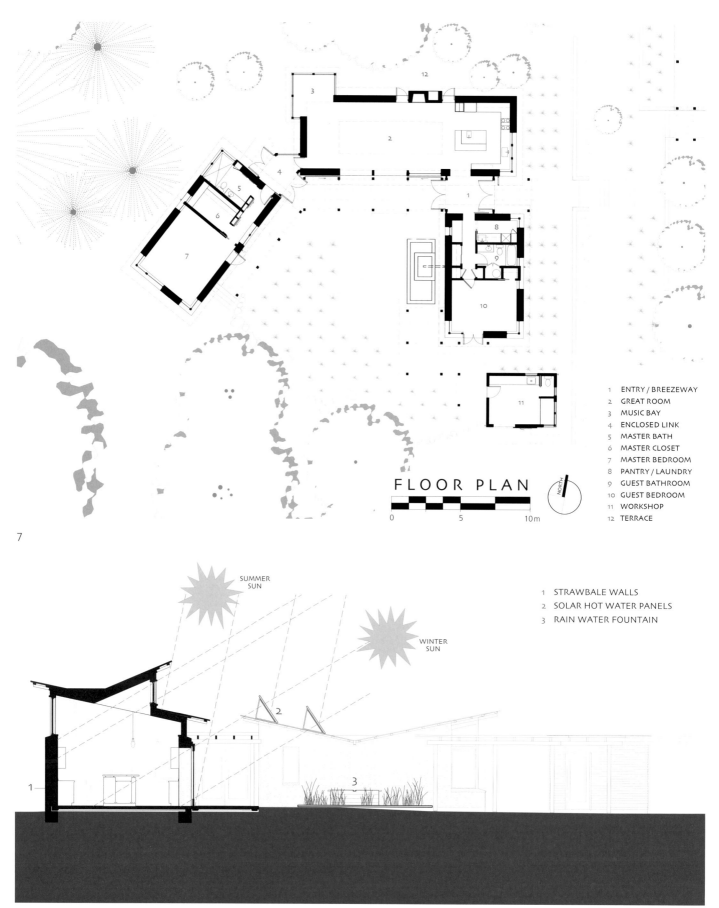

FLOOR PLAN

1 ENTRY / BREEZEWAY
2 GREAT ROOM
3 MUSIC BAY
4 ENCLOSED LINK
5 MASTER BATH
6 MASTER CLOSET
7 MASTER BEDROOM
8 PANTRY / LAUNDRY
9 GUEST BATHROOM
10 GUEST BEDROOM
11 WORKSHOP
12 TERRACE

0   5   10m

NORTH

7

SUMMER
SUN

WINTER
SUN

1 STRAWBALE WALLS
2 SOLAR HOT WATER PANELS
3 RAIN WATER FOUNTAIN

8

9

10

11

12

7 Floor plan

8 Section

9 Master bedroom

10, 11, 12 Interior views

Two-family home
Seeheim, Germany

Design: Benjamin Krick
Wall system: Timber skeleton with large bales attached outside
Completion: 2013
Floor area: 131 m² (56 m² ground floor, 75 m² first floor)

This passive house with two residential units is the extension of a two-family house from the 1960s. The self-bearing structure consists of timber framework with diagonal bracing. Jumbo bales laid on edge, with a thickness of 70 cm, a height of 120 cm and a length of up to 260 cm make up the exterior walls, which thus achieve a U-value of 0.08 W/(m²·K).

The bales weigh up to 300 kg and were connected in each course with the timber construction by a kind of horizontal "ladder", holding the bales in place. The bales were tied up into wall elements on a specially constructed "table" and then lifted by crane into their place in the wall. The roof was also covered with large bales. The walls have a fibre cement cladding on the outside and were rendered with earth plaster on the inside. Towards the south, the roof has 16 m² vacuum tube collectors and a 4.2 kWp photovoltaic system. The straw came from a field about 1 km away

and was delivered directly to the construction site. The required approx. 25 tonnes of straw cost approx. 2000 euros, including the delivery. The ceilings consist of fibre cement corrugated sheets. Reinforcing steel bars and pipes were alternately placed in the indentations of the corrugated sheet and then poured with concrete. Thus, the ceiling works as a heating surface. In the upper storey, which is partially open to the attic, pipes for heating were installed in the plaster of the walls. In summer, the heat surplus produced by the vacuum tube collectors is stored via a pipe register in the soil under the house. A horizontal insulating apron made of expanded glass gravel reduces the heat loss. For additional heating in winter, each room has a gas lamp that emits not only a pleasant light, but also provides a sufficiently cosy temperature. The CO_2 thus released into the room is channeled outside by the ventilation system.

1

2

3

4

5

6

7

8

1 Preparation of the jumbo bales on a "table"

2 The timber frame construction

3 Lifting of the 300 kg jumbo bale by crane

4, 5, 6, 8 Interior views

7 Exterior view

Single-family home
Stupava, Slovakia

Design: Createrra (Bjørn Kierulf and Marián Prejsa)
Wall system: Prefabricated timber elements with straw infill
Completion: 2013
Floor area: 99.5 m²

The compact two-storey house was planned as a passive house and was equipped with a forced ventilation with waste heat recovery system.

The loadbearing outer walls were assembled from prefabricated straw panels by the EcoCocon company. These elements are usually 1.20 m wide and have 45 × 90 mm wooden profiles at each of the four corners. Combined with the neighbouring stud they act as a column of 90 × 90 mm. Together, the profiles become a loadbearing timber structure. The elements are 40 cm wide and their straw bale surfaces were trimmed in the factory with a saw in order to achieve a smooth surface which was given a 2.5-cm-thick earth plaster on the inside. On the outside, a 10-cm-thick wood fibreboard insulation was installed which ensures that no condensation humidity can develop in the straw. On the ground floor, a mineral plaster and then a thin silicon render was applied to these fibreboards; on the top floor, a larch wood cladding was added. The roof was insulated with a 40-cm-thick layer of cellulose flakes and covered with vegetation.

To prevent the substrate of the green roof from slipping, horizontal aluminium profiles were fastened to the root-resistant roof sheathing as thresholds.

1

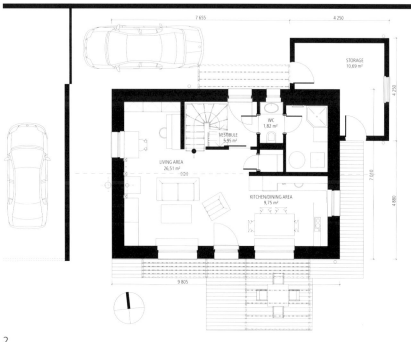

2

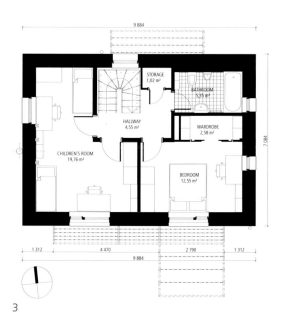

3

4

5

1 Corner detail with earth plaster

2 Ground floor plan

3 First floor plan

4 Exterior view with larch wood cladding on the upper storey

5, 6 Assembly of the prefabricated straw wall panels

6

Jules Ferry Résidence
St. Dié des Vosges, France

Design: ASP architecture
Energy concept: Terranergie
Wall system: CLT panels with straw infill in wooden boxes
Completion: 2013
Floor area: 2707 m²

The project is a three-storey and a seven-storey house with a total of 26 social housing units, each with 76 or 90 m² floor area. The loadbearing structure of the buildings consists of solid CLT panels. For thermal insulation, wooden boxes with the dimension 250 × 125 × 45 cm were filled with straw bales. The straw bales have a density of 135 kg/m³ and their strings were cut open after filling them into the boxes to ensure a tight connection with the wall. In front of the wooden elements a rear-ventilated brick panel façade was mounted to improve fire safety and rain protection. The roof is covered with 40-cm insulation layer of cellulose flakes. An exterior steel staircase and steel balconies create a visual contrast. Great care was taken to avoid any thermal bridges.

The energy concept comprises passive solar gain via the south façade, an active solar energy production over 50 m² collector area (used for hot water), as well as 12 geothermal energy probes and controlled ventilation via heat exchanger. Generally speaking, the concept prioritises the recovery of energy over the use of renewable energy which involves a mechanical ventilation double flow system and water heat recovery with an exchanger (powerpipe). The buildings achieve passive house standard.

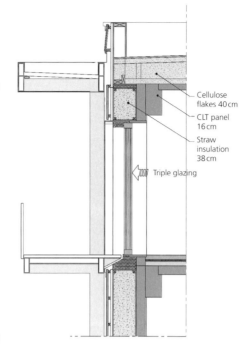

Cellulose flakes 40 cm
CLT panel 16 cm
Straw insulation 38 cm
Triple glazing

1

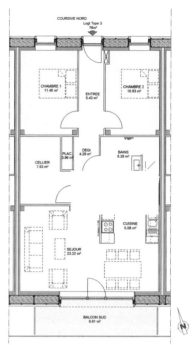

2

3

4

5

6

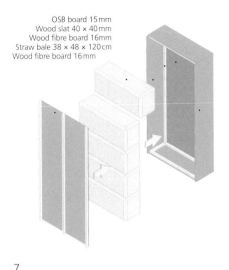

OSB board 15 mm
Wood slat 40 × 40 mm
Wood fibre board 16 mm
Straw bale 38 × 48 × 120 cm
Wood fibre board 16 mm

7

8

1 Façade section with steel balcony

2 Ground floor plan

3 Assembly of CLT walls on the foundation

4 Each storey was assembled with CLT panels and columns in the same way.

5 Montage of the insulation boxes in front of the CLT wall

6 Wooden insulation box filled with straw

7 Build-up of the wooden insulation element

8 Exterior view of the seven-storey building

9 Steel balcony with sunshade element

10 The CLT structure was left exposed inside.

9

10

Casa Muelle
Peñalolén, Santiago, Chile

Design: Nicole Spencer Chuaqui
Builder: Ayma Arquitectura y Medio Ambiente
Wall system: Timber frame skeleton with straw bale infill
Completion: 2014
Floor area: 230 m²

The Muelle residence, designed by the architect for herself, is located in the pre-cordilleras of Santiago, offering a beautiful view over the city. The foundation was made by reused car tires filled with dry sand and interconnected by steel bars. The exterior walls consist of a timber frame skeleton with straw bale infill to achieve good thermal insulation. For the interior walls, a wattle and daub system was used to provide sufficient thermal mass. All walls have an earth plaster from both sides and roofs are covered with earth and vegetation. Black and grey water is recycled and used for irrigation.

1

2

3

4

1 View over vegetation roof

2, 3 Exterior views

4 Interior

Residence on Mount Rankin
Bathurst, NSW, Australia

Design: six b design, Jamie Brennan
Builder: Madik Constructions
Straw contractor: Huff 'n' Puff
Constructions
Wall system: Timber frame with prefabricated jumbo bale infill
Completion: 2018
Floor area: 180 m²

The residence on Mount Rankin is a solar, passive, three-bedroom, single-storey house on a rural property not far from the city of Bathurst. The project is not connected to any mains services. Electric energy solar voltaic panels collect electric energy and store it in batteries for all electrical needs. Hydronic slab heating and cooling is used in the floor via a heat pump and geothermal ground coils. All roof water is collected and stored in a metal water tank for all in-house water use. Wastewater is treated by a reedbed system and disposed in the ground via rubble trenches.
Roof overhangs are designed to allow for maximum solar access in winter, while blocking the sun in summer. The floors and central internal wall are concrete and serve as internal thermal mass to store daytime solar heat for colder nights in winter and maintain cooler internal temperatures in the summer. The roof insulation, achieves a U-value of 0.25 W/(m²·K), to minimise heat loss and gain. The north and east walls are mainly of glass to maximise solar access in the morning and midday. Straw insulation of the south and west walls minimises heat loss to the south and afternoon heat gain. The straw bale walls where built up by prefabricated panels of structural plywood frames filled with straw bales ("Tilt-up panel system" by Huff 'n' Puff Constructions) and then covered by a lime plaster.

1

2

3

4

5

6

7

1 Delivery of prefabricated panels to the site

2, 3 Erection of the structural plywood frames with straw bale infill

4–7 Exterior views

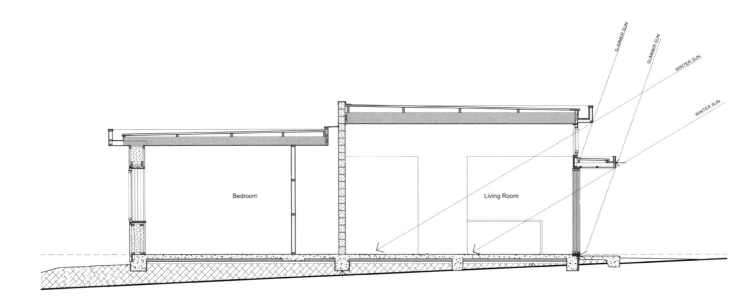

8

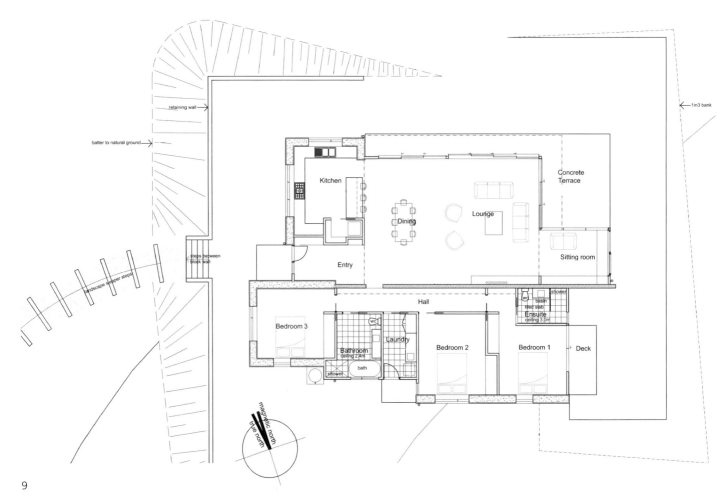

9

10

12

11

13

8 Cross section
9 Ground floor plan
10–13 Interior views

Pisa House
Wanaka, New Zealand

Design: Hiberna Ltd, Jessica Eyers
Construction: Hiberna Ltd, Ben Eyers
Engineering: eZED Ltd, Paula Hugens
Wall system: Timber skeleton with straw bale infill
Completion: 2019
Floor area: 120 m²

The two-storey family home was one of the first certified straw bale passive houses outside of Europe. The structure consists of an isolated slab on 200 mm of polystyrene, post-and-box beam wall structure on both storeys and a framed roof. The plasters are from earth and lime with some fibres from a paper mill. The windows are triple-glazed with timber frame. The ground floor was rendered with earth and the upper floor clad with native red beech. Internal walls are timber frames with straw-clay infill for sound insulation. The house (SHD = 10 kWh/m² · a) is heated by two 1 kW radiators, which are fed via a "scavenging" coil in the hot water cylinder, which is heated by a heat pump. The house generates 3 kWp with solar photovoltaic panels which powers the house and also charges the family's electric car.

1

2

1 Bedroom
2 Bathroom
3 Exterior view
4 Cross sections AA (left) and BB (right)

3

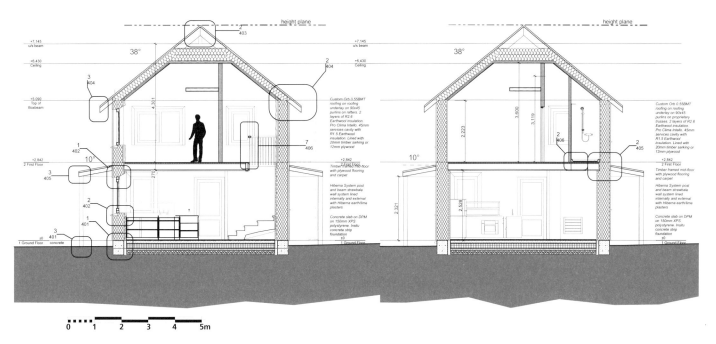

height plane

+7.145
u/s beam

38°

+6.430
Ceiling

+5.090
Top of
Boxbeam

3
404

1
402

10°

3
405

2
402

3
401

1
401

+2.842
2 First Floor

t0
1 Ground Floor   concrete

2
403

2
404

7
406

Custom Orb 0.55BMT
roofing on roofing
underlay on 90x45
purlins on rafters. 2
layers of R2.6
Earthwool insulation.
Pro Clima Intello. 45mm
services cavity with
R1.5 Earthwool
insulation. Lined with
20mm timber sarking or
12mm plywood

Timber framed mid-floor
with plywood flooring
and carpet

Hiberna System post
and beam strawbale
wall system lined
internally and external
with Hiberna earth/lime
plasters

Concrete slab on DPM
on 150mm XPS
polystyrene. Insitu
concrete strip
foundation

height plane

+7.145
u/s beam

38°

+6.430
Ceiling

10°

+2.842
2 First Floor

t0
1 Ground Floor

2
406

2
405

Custom Orb 0.55BMT
roofing on roofing
underlay on 90x45
purlins on proprietary
trusses. 2 layers of R2.6
Earthwool insulation.
Pro Clima Intello. 45mm
services cavity with
R1.5 Earthwool
insulation. Lined with
20mm timber sarking or
12mm plywood

Timber framed mid-floor
with plywood flooring
and carpet

Hiberna System post
and beam strawbale
wall system lined
internally and external
with Hiberna earth/lime
plasters

Concrete slab on DPM
on 150mm XPS
polystyrene. Insitu
concrete strip
foundation

0   1   2   3   4   5m

4

5

7

6

8

5 Insulated double bottom plate with first bale

6 Connection of first floor joists to wall

7 Exterior view

9

8 Strawbale walls with additional insulation at window openings to minimise thermal bridging

9 Window detail

10 First floor plan

11 Ground floor plan

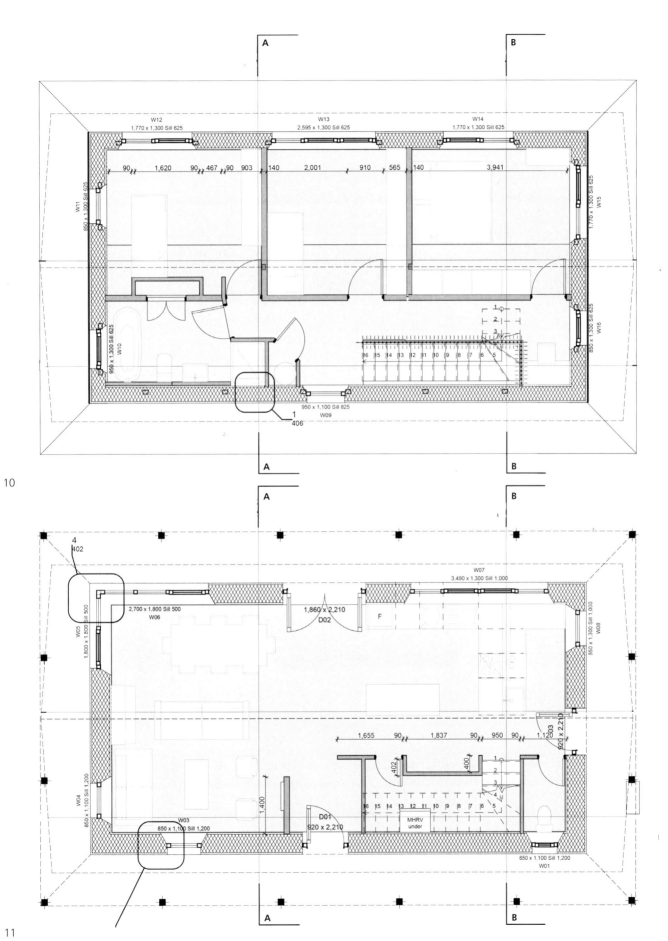

W12
1,770 x 1,300 Sill 625

W13
2,595 x 1,300 Sill 625

W14
1,770 x 1,300 Sill 625

90   1,620   90 467 90   903 140   2,001   910 565 140   3,941

W11
850 x 1,300 Sill 625

1,770 x 1,300 Sill 625
W15

850 x 1,300 Sill 625
W16

950 x 1,300 Sill 625
W10

1
2
3
4
5

16 15 14 13 12 11 10 9 8 7 6 5

950 x 1,100 Sill 825
W09

1
406

A   B

10

A   B

4
402

W05
1,800 x 1,800 Sill 500

2,700 x 1,800 Sill 500
W06

W07
3,490 x 1,300 Sill 1,000

1,860 x 2,210
D02

F

850 x 1,300 Sill 1,000
W08

W04
850 x 1,100 Sill 1,200

1,655   90   1,837   90 950 90   1,120

920 x 2,210
D03

402

400

1,400

1
2
3
4
5

W03
850 x 1,100 Sill 1,200

D01
920 x 2,210

16 15 14 13 12 11 10 9 8 7 6 5

MHRV
under

650 x 1,100 Sill 1,200
W01

A   B

11

Residential and office building
London, United Kingdom

Design and site supervision: Sarah Wigglesworth
Straw bale works: Scott Clark
Wall system: Partly loadbearing, partly primary timber frame with straw infill panels
Completion: 2001
Living area: 264 m²
Office area: 210 m²

The residential and office building is situated at the end of a street in a former industrial estate of London, hemmed in between rail tracks and small Victorian railway cottages. One leg of the L-shaped building houses an office, the other accommodates the residential wing. A room that can equally be used as meeting room and dining room links the two wings. The five-storey tower establishes the building as a visible landmark.

Strictly speaking, the building is not a pure straw bale structure, as straw bales were not used consistently throughout the building; instead, a mix of various building methods and materials was chosen. However, all methods ensured that materials came from sustainable sources and that their incorporated energy was low. Hence, recycled concrete was used just as well as sand bags filled with cement, lime and sand: the mixture will harden over time and – as the organic textile fibres decompose – it will reveal a coarse concrete finish.

The sleeping area was insulated with straw bales sitting between latticed timber posts. They are visible between the polycarbonate cladding, which is ventilated to ensure that condensation will not damage the bales. By means of this constructional device, the straw bales could be exposed and protected at the same time. On the inside, the straw bales are lime-rendered. The type of insulation used ensures that the heating period for these spaces is restricted to just a few weeks during winter.

1

2

3

1, 2, 3 Views of meeting/dining room

4 On the exterior, the straw bales are visible behind the polycarbonate cladding.

5 Kitchen

6 Stair to upper storey

7 The exterior with five-storey tower at dusk

4

5

6

7

Residential building
Langtaufers, Italy

Design and construction management for straw bale construction:
Atelier Werner Schmidt
Wall system: Loadbearing jumbo straw bales
Completion: 2008
Floor area: 300 m², with mezzanine 400 m²

The three-and-a-half-storey loadbearing straw bale house near Graun in South Tyrol accommodates two holiday apartments and a studio. A mezzanine on the upper floor adds another 100 m² of floor area. The walls are 120-cm-thick horizontal jumbo straw bales. The pyramid-shaped roof construction is made of wood and is insulated with 70-cm-thick jumbo bales. The walls have lime plaster on the outside, earth plaster on the inside. The heating demand is only approx. 20 kWh/m²·a. The top storey is daylit by a glazed roof and houses the studio for the artist client. The roof was clad by wood shingles.

1

2

1 Exterior view

2 The artist's studio under construction

3 Interior of the holiday apartment

4, 5, 6, 7 Construction sequence: the walls with straw bale infill are erected; the pyramid-shaped roof construction is added, the lower part of the roof is insulated with straw bales, the top part is glazed and the exterior is clad with shingles.

8 The construction site in its Alpine surroundings

3

4

6

7

5

8

Seminar and Office Buildings for Nature Centre Prenzlau, Germany

Design, structural design and construction management: STROH unlimited, Friederike Fuchs, Britta Imhoff
Wall system: Timber structure with straw bale infill
Completion: 2008
Floor area office building: 78 m²
Floor area seminar building: 80 m²

The two buildings of the "Naturerlebnis Uckermark", a nature centre addressing children and families in Prenzlau, were built with vertical timber studs and upright straw bales as infill. The bales were plastered with clay on the inside and with lime on the outside. The roof insulation consists of hemp wool. The construction works were done by 20 previously unemployed women and men as part of a qualification measure. The office space with café has an oval floor plan while the seminar building has a rectangular floor plan and is covered by an arched roof with a pyramid-shaped skylight.

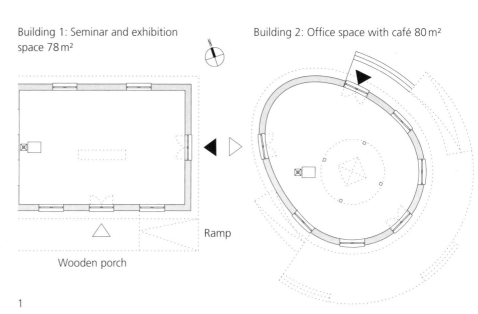

Building 1: Seminar and exhibition space 78 m²

Building 2: Office space with café 80 m²

Ramp

Wooden porch

1

2

3

4

5

6

1 Ground floor plan
2 Exterior of office building
3 Seminar building under construction
4 Office building roof under construction
5 Interior of office building with skylight
6 Interior view

Residence with office
Bad König, Germany

Design: Susanne Körner, Tilman Schäberle (Shakti Haus)
Straw bale works: Cato Räuchle, self-building by client
Wall system: Timber structure with straw bale infill
Completion: 2009
Floor area: approx. 240 m²

Susanne Körner and Tilman Schäberle are the partners of the architectural office Shakti Haus and created in Bad König in the Odenwald region their own place of residence and work. The building is a post-and-beam structure and achieved the German KfW 40 energy standard by integrating vertical straw bales as insulation. The roof and one of the outer walls are curved.

The interior finish of the bales is clay plaster and, to a lesser extent, OSB panels and gypsum fibreboards with clay plaster. On the exterior, a three-layer lime plaster was applied. A solar system prepares the hot water and contributes to the heating, aided by a wood gasification boiler.

1

2

1, 2 Roof installation
3 Ground floor plan
4 First floor plan
5 Second floor plan
6 Post-and-beam structure with straw bales partially in place
7 Exterior view

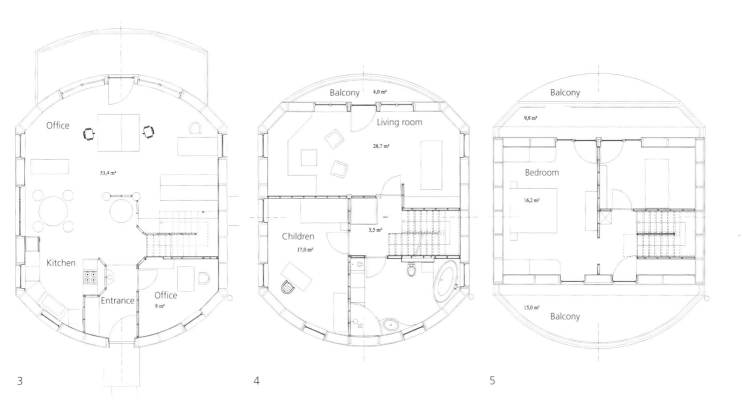

3

4

5

6

7

S-House
Böheimkirchen, Austria

Design: Georg Scheicher, GrAT (Vienna University of Technology)
Wall system: Solid timber walls with outside straw bale insulation
Completion: 2005
Floor area: approx. 332 m²

This project, which accommodates office space and a showroom, is a passive house that almost exclusively uses renewable building materials. The goal was a reduction of resource consumption compared to conventional buildings by a factor of 10. The structure comprises of walls and floors made of 10 cm KLH solid timber plates and was erected on point foundations raised above the ground. The floating roof construction is not supported by the walls. This allowed the whole building to be surrounded by a 50-cm-thick straw bale insulation layer. The bales sit on a cantilevered floor plate and were fastened to the wall construction by wooden dowels and hemp cords. On the outside, a rear-ventilated wooden façade was attached using the Treeplast straw screw while avoiding thermal bridges. A 2-cm-thick layer of clay plaster serves as a wind brake, protects against moisture and improves the fire protection properties of the wall construction. The clay used for the plaster came from the excavated material of the point foundations.

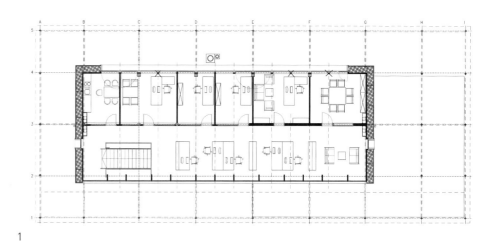

1

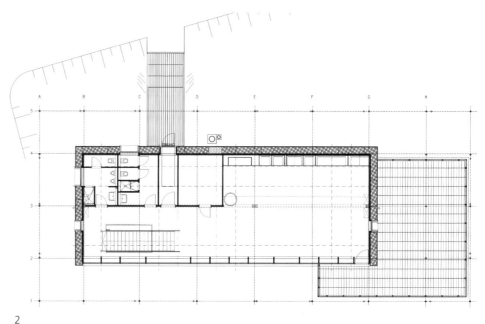

2

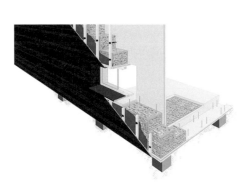

3

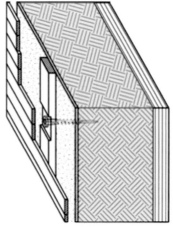

4

Horizontal boarding	20 mm
Ventilation cavity/counter battens attached with Treeplast screws	50 mm
Earth plaster	20 mm
Straw bale	500 mm
KLH solid timber plate	106 mm
Total	**696 mm**

U-value: 0.08 W/(m² · K)

5

6

7

8

1 First floor plan

2 Ground floor plan

3 Axonometric showing wall construction

4 Wall section with all components from the outside (left) to the inside (right)

5 Exterior view with porch

6 The wall with straw bale insulation layer partially installed

7 The building is raised above the ground by point foundations.

8 Wooden dowels are driven into the wall construction.

Single-family home with workshop
Knutwil, Switzerland

Design: Atelier Werner Schmidt
Project architect: Michael Schneider
Wall system: Prefabricated timber frame elements with straw bale infill
Completion: 2012
Floor area: 217 m²

The time between the start of earthworks on the site to completion of the building was only three months, enabled by element construction. The exterior walls consist of 70-cm-thick box elements made of wood, filled with large straw bales. On the outside a rear-ventilated spruce boarding, which has been painted red, provides weather protection. The inner layer of the exterior walls as well as the inside walls consist of 10-cm-thick cross-laminated wood panels. The roof, which was also made of prefabricated box elements, is covered with a green roof. Water is heated by 10 m² of solar panels and a pellet stove serves as emergency heating. The building site is a steep slope and the lower storey accommodates a workshop.

1

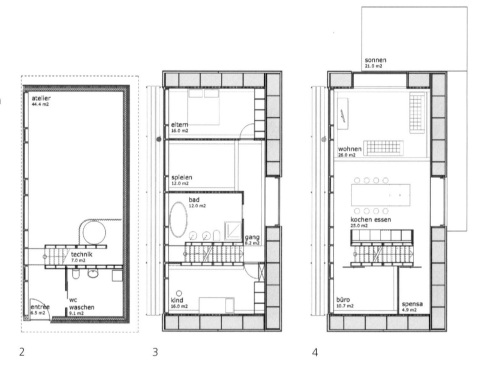

2   3   4

1 Front façade with lower storey which accommodates a workshop
2 Basement plan
3 Ground floor plan
4 First floor plan
5 Cross section
6 Longitudinal section
7 Assembly of wooden trusses
8 Wooden box element with straw bale infill
9 The house with surroundings
10 Rear façade
11 Living area
12 Dining area with pellet stove

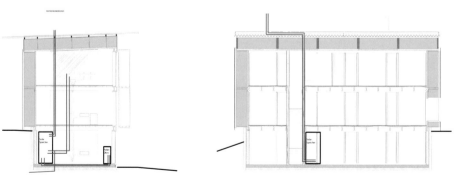

5   6

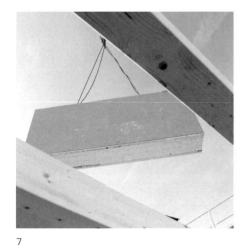

7

8

9

10

11

12

North German Center for Sustainable Building
Verden, Germany

Design: Architekten für Nachhaltiges Bauen, Frido Elbers, Thomas Isselhard, Dirk Scharmer
Completion: 2015
Floor area: 1780 m² with 500 m² exhibition area

The competence center of the North German Center for Sustainable Building includes a large exhibition area as well office and seminar spaces.

The basement walls consist of highly insulated, vertically perforated bricks, the load-bearing walls from the ground floor to the fourth are part of a timber post-and-beam structure, which has been assembled from 48-cm-thick wooden box elements filled with straw bales. The straw bales were covered on the outside with a three-layer lime plaster, on the inside the wall has two layers of gypsum plaster fire protection boards covered with earth plaster. The ceilings are made of 24-cm-thick nail laminated timber. The roof received extensive planting. The building meets the passive house standard. Vacuum tube collectors ensure solar energy coverage of 93 %. The remaining 7 % are delivered by a micro heat and power plant. Ventilation systems with waste heat recovery are part of the energy concept. In order to achieve plus energy standard, a 170 m² field of photovoltaic collectors with 20 kWp was installed on top of the fifth floor. All lighting in the building is via LED.

1

2

3

4

5

6

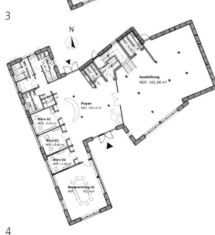

7

8

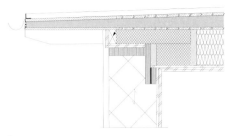

9

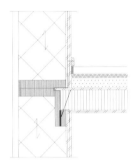

10

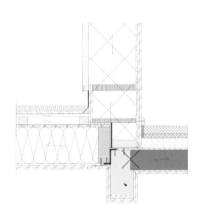

11

12

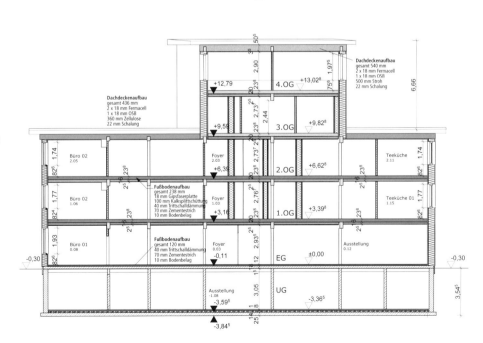

13

1 Third floor plan

2 Second floor plan

3 First floor plan

4 Ground floor plan

5 Base plate consisting of hollow blocks

6 The wall elements with timber boards, straw bales and an OSB board as bracing were assembled close to the site.

7 Transport of wall elements

8 The prefabricated and lime-rendered wall elements are lifted into place.

9 Detail section showing wall-roof connection

10 Detail section of floor slab support

11 Detail section showing wall-floor connection

12 Exterior view

13 View of exhibition space

14 West-east section

14

Office building
Tattendorf, Austria

Design: Georg W. Reinberg, Roland Meingast
Wall system: Prefabricated elements with straw bale infill in timber skeleton
Completion: 2006
Floor area: 360 m²

The building in Tattendorf is a passive house insulated with straw. The walls are one-storey-high prefabricated elements that were assembled into a timber structure. The interior and exterior surfaces of these elements were earth-plastered. The base floor slab and the roof slab also consist of prefabricated, straw-insulated elements. The straw bales were installed with a special compactor. The elements were delivered by train and moved with the help of a mobile crane. The airtight layer consists of a special reinforced earth plaster. The joints between the elements were covered with a non-woven that was plastered with earth which "glued" the fabric to the joint and thus achieved airtightness.

The building was covered with a green roof. Thermal insulation and all building components comply with "Passive House Standards". The supply air is channeled through an underground duct and thus preconditioned and an air heat exchanger with heat recovery reduces ventilation heat losses. The air flow inside the building is conducted through earthen hollow bodies. The residual heat requirement is covered by the hot water collectors on the façade and auxiliary heating is provided by bio-ethanol (which can also be used to humidify indoor air). Photovoltaic cells on the south façade provide the total auxiliary power requirement. The roof is designed as a bat nesting site.

1

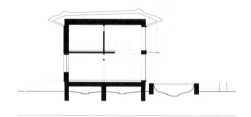

2

3

4

5

6

1 In winter, the façade allows for solar gain and ample daylight.

2 Lighting concept in summer

3 The straw insulation is filled into the wall elements and then compacted.

4 Exterior view

5 Prefabricated wall elements moved by train and crane to the building site

6 The roof slab is installed.

Living vaults
Tamera, Portugal

Design: Gernot Minke
Construction management: Beate Möller, Gernot Minke
Workshop management: Gernot Minke with Dittmar Hecken, Benjamin Krick, Alfonso Lipardi, Paul Wyser
Wall system: Loadbearing vault
Completion: 2007
Floor area per unit: 17 m², plus 5.5 m² covered terrace

1

The three "living vaults" in the peace community of Tamera near Colos were the first loadbearing straw bale vaults. They consist of conically cut bales assembled in the structurally optimal form of a catenary arch. For trimming the bales, which have a different conical form in each layer, a cutting device developed at the Research Laboratory for Experimental Building (FEB) at the University of Kassel was used.

The bales were placed over a formwork piled up without mortar. After the top bales were inserted the vaults were slightly pre-tensioned by webbing straps. After removing the formwork the vault only decreased in height by less than 1 mm.

On the outside, the vaults received two layers of earth plaster, and three layers were applied on the inside. The vaults are covered with a bituminous membrane and a green roof with thyme, other wild herbs and grasses on approx. 15 cm of soil.

The valleys between the vaults were filled with cork waste from the neighbouring cork oak forests and with plastic waste containers filled with clay mortar, to reduce the lateral loadings on the vault. The end faces of the barrels were clad with natural

2

stones that were left over on the site from the earthworks for a nearby road.

The north façade consists of upright straw bales, the south façade is predominantly double glazing. The wall areas next to the entrance glazing were filled with cotton tubing stuffed with light clay, fixed with bamboo sticks during the construction. In the base area of the walls, plastic pipes were integrated in the earth plaster. They conduct water, which has been heated by solar panels, for heating in the winter. The windows allow for natural ventilation which lets in cooler air at night, thus cooling the room in summer. The roof overhang at the entrance terrace also helps to avoid solar gain during the hot season.

The three vaults were built in a three-week workshop with 25 participants from ten countries.

The cost of materials and transportation amounted to approx. 4300 euros per unit plus about 1200 euros for solar heating. During the workshop, there were 16 working days with approx. 2000 working hours. The remaining work required approx. 400 more hours.

3

4

5

6

8

7

1 Trimming of bales by a specially developed cutting device

2 Straps are used for pretensioning the vaults.

3 The top conical bale is fitted into the arch.

4 Exterior view

5 Interior view

6 The exterior of the vaults is covered by two layers of earth plaster.

7 Bamboo sticks were used for support during the construction.

8 The bales are placed on formwork.

Accommodation vaults
Buchberg-Wangelin, Germany

Design: Gernot Minke, Tobias Weyhe
Workshop management: Gernot Minke
with Dittmar Hecken, Isabelle Melchior,
Catarina Pinto, Ana Ruivo
Wall system: Loadbearing straw bale
vaults
Completion: 2013
Floor area: 143 m²

The building serves the non-profit association FAL e.V. and the Europäische Bildungsstätte für Lehmbau (www.earth-building.eu) as overnight accommodation for seminar participants and lecturers. It is meant to serve as an example of a sustainable building using natural materials that can be realised with low cost, given a high degree of self-building and voluntary work. The construction was supported by the European Agricultural Fund for Rural Development (EAFRD). It was the first loadbearing vault building made from straw bales that received a building permit in Germany. A 50-cm-thick layer of compressed foam glass gravel serves as foundation, interrupting capillary forces and providing thermal insulation.
The barrels were made of conically cut straw bales without mortar, erected above a formwork and poststressed with tensioned straps. After removal of the straps,

no settlement occurred. The vaults received a three-layer earth plaster on the inside and outside. The green roof consists of a root barrier membrane, 12-cm lightweight substrate and a vegetation layer with wild grasses and herbs. When installed, the straw bales had an equilibrium moisture of 15 %. The 6- to 8-cm-thick external plaster warrants that even in winter and 40 % relative humidity in the interior the dew point remains in the earth layer, but not in the straw. For the third interior render layer, 6 % linseed oil varnish was added to the mixture so that this layer acts as vapour barrier. The moisture behaviour within the vaults is monitored by 12 sensors. Part of the construction work such as cutting, mounting, post-stressing and plastering of bales, as well as the rammed earth floor and the interior design with loam-filled cotton tubes, were done within two international workshops of one week each.

▨	Aerated concrete wall
▨	Straw bales on aerated concrete base
▨	Rammed earth wall

▨	Straw bales on aerated concrete base
▨	Rammed earth wall
▦	Substrate green roof
▨	Aerated concrete wall
▨	Foam glass gravel

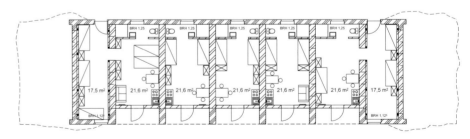

1

2

3

4

5

6

7

8

9

1 Ground floor plan

2 Section

3 Exterior view

4 Sawing the bales into the right shape

5, 6 Mounting the bales on top of the vault

7 Post-stressing of the bales

8 Application of the earth plaster

9 Cotton tubes filled with loam are used in the bedroom.

Office Building
Hrubý Šúr, Slovakia

Design: Gernot Minke
Detail design: Bjørn Kierulf, Createrra
Workshop management: Gernot Minke with Pierre Bortnowski, Samuel Gros, Olaf Eggers, Dittmar Hecken, Stefan Ohnesorg, Pavel Pakuza
Earth plaster: Piet Karlstedt
Wall system: Loadbearing straw bale vaults and dome
Completion: 2011
Floor area: 62 m²

In Hrubý Šúr, a small place nearby Bratislava, the world's first loadbearing straw bale dome was built. It consists of eight loadbearing straw bale vaults, covered by a vegetation roof.

The building has a central octagonal space for seminars and exhibitions which is surrounded by eight vaults, each with a 4 m² niche that accommodates office workplaces and a tea kitchen. The building is home to the architectural office of Createrra, leading Passivhaus specialist in Slovakia. The central area is covered with a dome that has a clear diameter of 6.20 m and rests on an octagonal ring beam. This ring beam is supported by eight round 30-cm-thick wooden posts. The straw bales, which have a cross section of 36 × 48 cm, were cut conically on both sides with a saw that was developed by the Research Laboratory for Experimental Building (FEB) at the University of Kassel. The device has two saw blades, whose inclination can be adjusted with an accuracy of 0.5 degree. Thus, flat bale surfaces can be achieved and the straw bales can be placed directly on top of each other without mortar, avoiding open joints. When making the dome, the bales had to be bent to form an arch. The bales of the eight vaults were erected above formwork. The dome, however, was built without formwork but aided by a rotation guide developed by FEB that held the bale in the correct position until it was stabilised by wooden pins.

Vaults and dome were covered inside and outside by 5 cm of earth plaster, applied in three layers on either side. The "valleys" between the vaults on the exterior were filled with straw bales and with bags stuffed with foam glass gravel.

The roof was covered with an EPDM roof membrane. To prevent the substrate from sliding, it was put in polyethylene bags. These bags were then stacked and sprinkled with wild grass seeds.

The rammed earth floor was insulated with 50 cm expanded glass gravel and the façade with 30 cm cellulose flakes. The vault cross section with 36 cm upright straw bales, 2 × 5 cm clay plaster, 12 cm substrate and vegetation layer has an U-value of 0.134 W/(m²·K), while near the filled "valleys" an U-value of approx. 0.08 W/(m²·K) is achieved. The windows have a three-layer glazing, the acrylic glass skylight dome has a four-layer glazing. Even if the outside temperature drops to -11 °C, only 1600 W of heating power is needed.

The supply air is warmed up by the exhaust air in a heat exchanger and channeled through the ring beam, which also serves as an air duct, to the eight vaults. The roof structure does not comprise an internal vapour barrier because it was assumed that the outer earth plaster layer would sufficiently absorb condensation humidity in the winter and then release it again during the summer.

To monitor the moisture in the straw, 12 sensors were installed. Measurements after three years showed that the humidity inside the bales did not exceed 14 %. The building was realised during two workshops of two weeks each.

1

2

3

4

5

6

7

1 Conically cut bales on formwork

2 Shrinkage cracks are being refilled

3 Plastering of the interior surfaces of the vaults

4 Interior view

5 The dome under construction covered with earth-filled bags

6 The building with vegetation in summer after one year

7 The building in winter

Foothills Academy College Preparatory
Scottsdale, Arizona, USA

Design: Weddle + Gilmore Architects
Site supervision: Tom Hahn, Three Rivers EcoBuilders
Wall system: Steel and reinforced concrete frame with straw bale insulation and cement-based render
Completion: 2002
Floor area: 2050 m²

At the time of its completion, the Foothills private college preparatory with a size of 2000 m² was one of the largest straw bale buildings worldwide. Buildings containing classrooms as well as a media centre and administrative offices are grouped around a central square, which is also used as an outdoor classroom.

Located at the banks of an existing riverbed, the design ensured that the natural waterways were not altered or disturbed. The scheme respects the character of the surrounding landscape and the natural vegetation. Rainwater is collected and recycled for irrigation.

The large glazed areas of the building comply with passive solar design principles and ensure sufficient solar gains during winter. Large roof overhangs prevent overheating during summer. The building's mechanical engineering such as water-saving technology and natural ventilation is likewise designed to minimise negative impact on the environment.

The building structure consists of steel and reinforced concrete columns, which are insulated with straw bales. They are connected to each other and to the roof with metal pins. The walls were rendered with cement-based and acrylic-modified stucco.

1

2

3

4

5

6

1 At the corners the concrete columns are partially left exposed.

2 The interior under construction

3, 4 Exterior views: the large roof overhangs prevent overheating.

5 Corner details

6 The roof is supported by metal pins.

Nalawala Community Hall
Fairfield, Sydney, Australia

Design: Tracy Graham
Engineer: Morse McVey and Associates
Builder: Huff 'n' Puff Constructions
Wall system: Loadbearing jumbo straw bale walls
Floor area: 290 m²
Completion: 2008

The Fairfield Community Hall is part of the Fairfield Showgrounds, a regional multi-cultural and sporting complex in Western Sydney, that was subsequently redeveloped in 2018/2019. The community facility is also called the Nalawala Hall ("sit down" in one of the Aboriginal languages) and was built with straw bale walls on a recycled concrete slab foundation. Also the kitchen was second hand and doors and floors were recycled as well. Generally speaking, the hall was designed on passive design principles including orientation for winter solar gain, summer shading, cross ventilation, thermal mass, insulation and appropriate glazing. Low embodied energy construction has been embraced with the straw bale walls and an all-timber structure.

Additional sustainability features of the project include a worm farm composting system, wastewater treatment, rainwater collection, coupled with a solar hot water system, photovoltaic panels, low-energy lighting and roof ventilators. The high insulation characteristics of the straw bale walls reduce the energy demands of the building. For the loadbearing walls jumbo straw bales measuring 2.4 × 0.9 × 0.6 m, weighing 250 kg each, were put into place using a forked tractor. The non-loadbearing, smaller bales measuring 0.9 × 0.45 × 0.35 m were put up manually with some community help. All walls were compressed using threaded rods fixed to foundation and roof plate and rendered with three coats of lime plaster.

1

1, 4 Entrance
2, 3, 5 External views

2

3

4

5

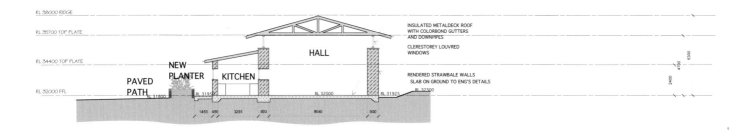

RL 38000 RIDGE
RL 35700 TOP PLATE
RL 34400 TOP PLATE
RL 32000 FFL

PAVED PATH
NEW PLANTER
KITCHEN
HALL

RL 31800
RL 31950
RL 32000
RL 31925
RL 32300

1453 450 3291 900 8040 900

INSULATED METALDECK ROOF WITH COLORBOND GUTTERS AND DOWNPIPES
CLERESTOREY LOUVRED WINDOWS
RENDERED STRAWBALE WALLS SLAB ON GROUND TO ENG'S DETAILS

6300 4700 2400

6

BOUNDARY

RL 38000 RIDGE
RL 35700 TOP PLATE
RL 34400 TOP PLATE
RL 32000 FFL

POLYTUNNEL
WC
HALL
NEW GARDEN

BOUNDARY
EXISTING TREES

INSULATED METALDECK ROOF WITH COLORBOND GUTTERS AND DOWNPIPES
RENDERED STRAWBALE WALLS SLAB ON GROUND TO ENG'S DETAILS

5137 452 3546 900 16597 900 4253

6300 4700 2400

7

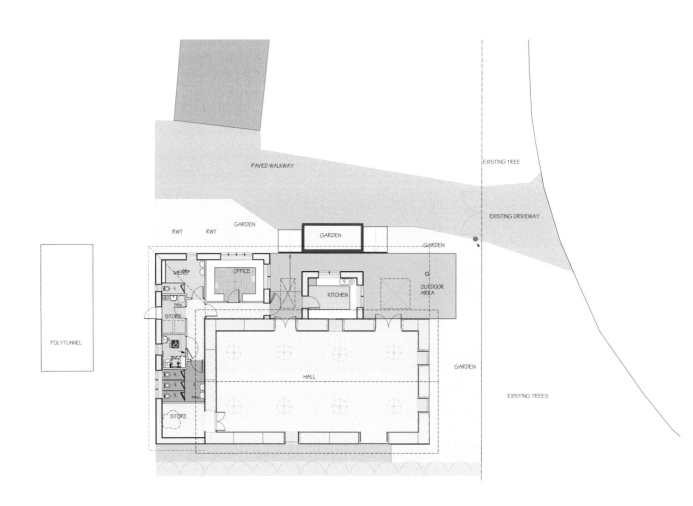

PAVED WALKWAY
EXISTING TREE
EXISTING DRIVEWAY
GARDEN
RWT RWT GARDEN
GARDEN
MENS
OFFICE
KITCHEN
GARDEN
OUTDOOR AREA
STORE
FWa
HALL
GARDEN
POLYTUNNEL
STORE
FWa
EXISTING TREES

8

9

10

11

6 Cross section

7 Longitudinal section

8 Ground floor plan

9 Construction of the wall

10, 11 Views of the hall interior

12 Entrance to the hall

13 Kitchen

12

13

Kindlehill Highschool
Wentworth Falls, NSW, Australia

Design: Sunlab Architecture with six b design, Simon Hearn and Jamie Brennan
Engineer: Ian Hayes
Wall system: Timber post-and-beam structure with straw bale infill
Completion: 2010
Floor area: approx. 450 m²

The form of this Rudolf Steiner school in the Blue Mountains was derived from the nautilus shell and the building has the shape of an unfolding spiral. Sustainability was a priority and components such as doors and windows were reused from other sites; pine trees that had been cleared from the school grounds were used for the main timber frame structure, which was filled with straw bales. The earth for render and cob for the walls was drawn from an excavation site at the nearby grammar school. A conscious decision was made to use non-toxic and sustainable products only. Traditional timber framing of mortise and tenon joints was used along with straw bales and cob for the walls. This provided increased insulation against the cold as well as effective acoustics. Many volunteers visiting from other countries, found through a help exchange network, brought their hands-on enthusiasm to the building project, as did volunteers from the school and local community.

1

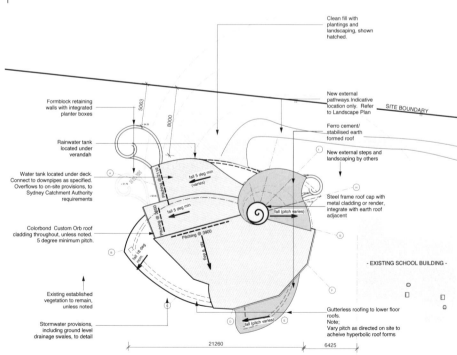

2

3

4

5

1 Exterior view
2 Site plan
3 Exterior view
4 Multi-purpose room with stage
5 Entrance

6

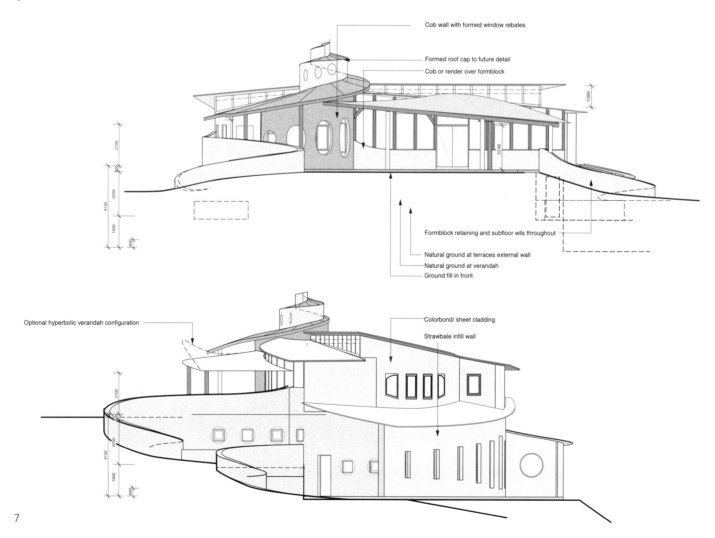

Cob wall with formed window rebates

Formed roof cap to future detail

Cob or render over formblock

Formblock retaining and subfloor wlls throughout

Natural ground at terraces external wall

Natural ground at verandah

Ground fill in front

Optional hyperbolic verandah configuration

Colorbond/ sheet cladding

Strawbale infill wall

7

8

9

10

6 Exterior view

7 North elevation (top) and west elevation (bottom)

8 Aerial view

9 Rooftop with clerestory

10 Rooftop from below

Training pavilion
Oensingen, Switzerland

Design: Atelier Werner Schmidt (project architect: Michael Schneider)
Wall system: Timber arches covered with straw bales
Completion: 2010
Floor area: 217 m²
Covered area: 812 m²

The dome-shaped pavilion is used by the company vonRoll hydro for training and exhibition purposes. The dome consists of 24 arched binders made from glue-laminated wood. The binders end at the top in a glue-laminated compression ring that supports a dome-shaped skylight. The timber construction has a straw bale infill and was given a lime render on the outside. Inside, 5-cm-thick mineral wool mats were attached to the walls. To the mats, a spray plaster with cotton and cellulose flakes was applied to improve noise protection. The lower part of the elliptical training room consists of three-layer glazing elements that form a 2.50-m-high wall. Inside the elliptical space a cube built with black MDF boards was inserted that accommodates sanitary rooms, kitchenette and storage. A curved membrane covering the dome and the surrounding spaces provides protection from the elements .

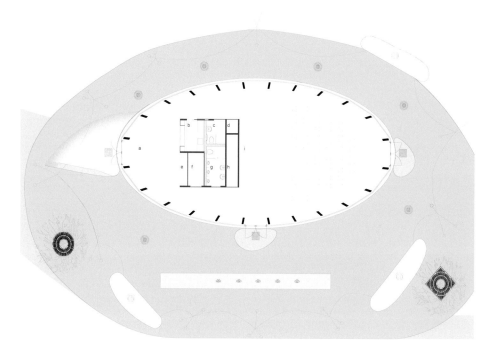

1   5   10m

1

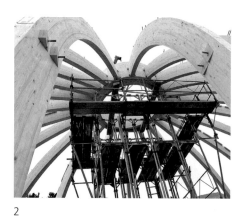

2

3

4

5

6

7

8

1 Ground floor plan

2, 3 Montage of the arched binders

4, 5 Installation of the straw bale infill between the rafters

6 Mounting of the exterior membrane

7, 8 Cube with kitchen and storage space in the interior

9 Exterior view at night

9

Montessori-Kindergarten
Catripulli, Chile

Design: Gernot Minke, Bruno Dezerega
Wall system: Timber post-and-beam structure with straw bale infill
Completion: 2019
Floor area: 122.5 m², covered area: 148 m²

The building is entered through a foyer, where the kids leave their shoes and jackets. At the core of the building is a central octagonal room without furniture, which is used for movement games, but also for cultural events in the evening or on weekends. This space is covered by a timber Hogan roof with a central skylight. Adjacent to the central space is an additional room of 21 m² with large windows to the outside. It has a large blackboard and can be separated from the central room by mobile elements or curtains for more quiet activities. The central room is surrounded by office, kitchen, reading room, toilets and a deposit space.

The foundation is a very economical earthquake-resistant solution created without using concrete: three layers of used car tires were filled with gravel and serve as a "floating foundation", which absorbs the kinetic energy of earthquake shockwaves by its ductility. 9000 non-recyclable plastic bottles, collected by the parents, serve as thermal insulation for the wooden floor. Walls consist of a timber post-and-beam structure with straw bale infill, which is covered by an earth plaster. The weather protection is provided by rough timber planks. The roof was covered by earth and grass sods of local wild grasses and herbs, with a total height of 15 cm.

The building was erected within five months' time only. The total building costs were about 80,000 USD, which translates into 540 USD/m² covered area, significantly less than the usual building costs for a kindergarten in Chile.

1

2

3

4

5

6

7

8

1 Mounting the vegetation roof

2 Ground floor plan

3 Laying the foundation

4 Plastic bottles serve as floor insulation.

5 Pressing the bales into the timber structure

6 Exterior view

7 Interior view

8 Ceiling with Hogan roof

Bibliography

AbZ 2006 – Deutsches Institut für Bautechnik (2006): Allgemeine bauaufsichtliche Zulassung Z-23.11-1595

Boye, Alan (2014): *Sustainable Compromises: A Yurt, a Straw Bale House, and Ecological Living.* University of Nebraska Press, Lincoln.

Büermann, Martin (1999): Mähdrescheruntersuchungen, Einflüsse auf die Kornabscheidung der Wendetrommel nachgeschalteter Abscheidetrommeln. In: *Landtechnik,* 1/1999.

Buydens, Sharon (2018): *DIY: How to Design Your Own Energy Efficient Green Home: Construction Alternatives and Sample Passive Solar Straw Bale House.* CreateSpace Independent Publishing Platform.

Buydens, Sharon (2018): *Cheapskate's Passive Solar Home Design for DIY Straw Bale or Green Building: Thrifty Ways to Barter and Find Cheap Used & Free Materials on a Frugal Budget.* CreateSpace Independent Publishing Platform.

CASBA: Straw Bale Building Details: An Illustrated Guide for Design and Construction (2019). New Society Publishers, Gabriola Island, British Columbia.

Danielewicz, I. and J. Reinschmidt (2007): "Lastversuche mit großen Quaderballen an der Hochschule Magdeburg-Stendal"

Doolittle, B. (1973): "A Round House of Straw Bales". In: *Mother Earth News,* 19, pp. 52–57.

Fachverband Strohballenbau Deutschland e. V. (FASBA), (ed.), (2008): Grundlagen zur bauaufsichtlichen Anerkennung der Strohballenbauweise –

Weiterentwicklung der lasttragenden Konstruktionsart und Optimierung der bauphysikalischen Performance. DBU Az. 22430.

FASBA: Strohbaurichtlinie 2019. http://fasba.de/wp-content/uploads/2019/10/FASBA-Strohbaurichtlinie-2019.pdf

Grandsaert, M. F. (1999): "A Compression Test of Plastered Straw-Bale Walls". University of Colorado at Boulder, USA.

GrAT (2001): Wimmer, R.; Hohensinner, H.; Janisch, L.; Drack, M.: Wandsysteme aus nachwachsenden Rohstoffen. Wirtschaftsbezogene Grundlagenstudie. Final report, "Gruppe Angepasste Technologie" (GrAT), Technical University Vienna.

Gruber, Herbert and Astrid, and Helmuth Santler (fourth edition, 2012): *Neues Bauen mit Stroh.* ökobuch Verlag, Staufen.

Jones, Barbara (2015): *Building with Straw Bales. A Practical Manual for Self-Builders and Architects.* Green Books, Cambridge, UK.

King, Bruce (ed.) (2006): *Design of Straw Bale Buildings,* The State of the Art. Green Building Press, San Rafael, CA.

Köhler/Klingele (eds.) (1995): "Baustoffdaten – Ökoinventare". Karlsruhe University.

Krick, Benjamin (2008): "Untersuchung von Strohballen und Strohballenkonstruktionen hinsichtlich ihrer Anwendung für ein energiesparendes Bauen unter besonderer Berücksichtigung der lasttragenden Bauweise". PhD thesis, University of Kassel, Kassel University Press.

Lacinski, Paul and Michel Bergeron (2000): *Serious Straw Bale – A Home Construction Guide for all Climates.* Chelsea Green Publishing, Hartford, Vermont.

Magwood, Chris and Peter Mack (2002): *Straw Bale Building.* New Society Publishers, Gabriola Island, British Columbia.

Magwood, Chris (2016): *Essential Prefab Straw Bale Construction: The Complete Step-by-Step Guide.* New Society Publishers, Gabriola Island, British Columbia.

McElderry, W. and C. (1979): "Happyness in a Hay House". In: *Mother Earth News,* 58, pp. 40–43.

Minke, Gernot (fifth edition, 2016): *Dächer begrünen. Einfach und wirkungsvoll.* ökobuch Verlag, Staufen

Minke, Gernot (third edition, 2013): *Building with Earth. Design and Technology of a Sustainable Architecture.* Birkhäuser, Basel

Règles Professionnelles de la construction en paille. Remplissage isolant et support d'enduit. (third edition, 2018), Le Moniteur, Paris.

Eisenberg, David and Martin Hamme (2014): "Strawbale Construction and Its Evolution in Building Codes". *Building Safety Journal Online,* February 2014, International Code Council.

Rijven, Tom (2008): *Between Earth and Straw.* Goutte de Sable, Athée.

Schmidt, Werner (2003): "Strohballendruckversuche". Atelier Werner Schmidt, Trun, Switzerland.

Sedlbauer, Klaus (2001): "Vorhersage von Schimmelpilzbildung auf und in Bauteilen". PhD thesis, University of Stuttgart.

Smith, Dan (2003): "Creep in Bale Walls". DSA Architects Berkeley.

Steen et. al. (1994): *The Straw Bale House.* Chelsea Green Publishing, Hartford, Vermont.

Strang, G. (1983): "Straw Bale Studio". In: *Fine Home Building,* 12/83, pp. 70–72.

Wedig, Harald (1999): GUS-Staaten, in: *Stroh im Kopf,* 1/1999, Xanten

Welsch, R. L. (1970): "Sandhill Baled Hay Construction". In: *Keystone Folklore Quarterly,* spring issue 1970, pp. 16–34.

Wihan, J. (2007): "Humidity in Straw Bale Walls and its Effect on the Decomposition of Straw". PhD thesis, University of East London.

Wimmer, R., H. Hohensinner and M. Drack (2006): *S-House, Innovative Nutzung von nachwachsenden Rohstoffen am Beispiel eines Büro- und Ausstellungs- gebäudes.* Bundesministerium für Verkehr, Innovation und Technologie, Vienna.

Zhang, John Q. and Michael Fine (2005): "Preliminary Discussion of Bale on Edge Wall Test". University of Western Sydney.

Illustration credits

Front cover: Straw bale house "Mühlen-hölzchen", Bad Belzig, Germany (Design: Dirk Hottelmann; planning and construction: Timo Brenner; photograph: Anando Arnold)
Back cover, from top to bottom:
Seminar building, Stollhof, Austria (Design: Georg W. Reinberg, Martha Enriquez Reinberg; photograph: Architek-turbüro Reinberg)
Casa Muelle, Santiago, Chile (Design: Nicole Spencer Chuaqui; photograph: Pablo Blanco)
Vine Hill Residence, Sonoma County, California, USA (Design: Arkin Tilt Archi-tects; photograph: Ed Caldwell)
Spiral House, Co. Mayo, Ireland (Design: Norita Clesham; photograph: Barbara Jones)

Architekturbüro Reinberg: 2.17; p. 134, 135 (1–6)
Architekten für Nachhaltiges Bauen: p. 132 (1–4); 133 (9–11, 14)
Arkin Tilt Architects: p. 100 (2); p. 102 (7, 8)
Blanco, Pablo: p. 110 (2); p. 111 (3, 4)
Caldwell, Ed: p. 100 (1); p. 101 (3–6); p. 103 (9–12)
ASP architecture: p. 108, 109 (1, 2, 7)
Atelier Werner Schmidt: 1.1; 8.5; p. 98, 99 (1–7); p. 122, 123 (1–8); p. 130, 131 (1–12); p. 152 (1)
Blöchl, Wolfgang: 11.7; 14.11
Claas: 3.1; 3.10
Clark, Dick: p. 144, 145 (1–5); p. 146 (6–8); p. 147 (9–13)
Createrra (Bjørn Kierulf): 141 (4–7)
Dalmeijer, René: 2.20
de Bouter, A.: 2.5
Degouda, Lucia: p. 152, 153 (2–9)
Dezerega, Bruno: p. 154 (2)
Downton, Paul: p. 90–93 (1–11)
Eisenberg, David: 2.1; 2.2; 2.3
Erz und Gugel: p. 96, 97 (1–10)
Eyers, Jessica (Hiberna Ltd.): pp. 116–119
FASBA 2008: 4.15
Frick, F.: 2.16
Fuchs, Friederike: 1.5–1.6; p. 124, 125 (1–6)
GrAT: 12.14
GrAT, Tagungsband Strohbau Symposium 2001: 2.6
Gruber, Santler, *Neues Bauen mit Stroh:* 2.7
Hahn, Tom: p. 142, 143 (1–6)
Hecken, Dittmar: p. 132 (5–8); p. 133 (13)
Heizmann, Oliver.: 8.8; 8.9
Henselmans, J.: 2.4
Hirrich, Klaus: p. 139 (3)
Huff 'n' Puff Constructions: 2.18
Janin, Arthur: p. 108, 109 (3–6, 8–10)
Jones, Barbara: 1.2
Kindle Hill School: p. 150 (6); p. 151 (8, 10)
Krick, Benjamin: 1.3; 2.19; 3.4; 3.5; 3.6; 3.7; 3.8; 3.9; 4.1; 4.2; 4.3; 4.4; 4.5; 4.6; 4.7; 4.8; 4.9; 4.10; 4.11; 4.13; 5.1; 5.2; 5.3; 6.1; 6.2; 6.3; 6.4; 6.5; 6.6; 6.7; 6.8; 6.9; 7.1; 8.1; 8.2; 8.7; 8.10; 9.7; 9.9; 11.3; 11.12; 11.14; 11.15; 11.16; p. 104, 105 (1–8)

Lacinski, Bergeron, 2000: 3.2
Mahlke, Friedemann: 10.1; 10.2; 10.3; 1.1; 11.2; 11.8; 11.9; 11.10; 11.11; 1.12; 11.13; 11.19; 11.20; 11.21; 11.22; 11.23; 11.24; 11.25; 11.26; 11.27; 11.28; 11.29; 11.30; 11.31; 11.32; 11.33; 11.34; 11.35; 11.36; 11.37; 11.38; 11.39; 11.40; 11.41; 11.42; 11.43; 14.1; 14.6
Marinica, D.: p. 106, 107 (1–6)
Millies, Frank: 14.7;
Minke, Gernot: 2.8; 2.11; 2.12; 2.13; 2.14; 2.15; 4.16; 4.17; 9.1; 9.2; 9.3; 9.4; 9.5; 9.6; 9.7; 9.8; 11.4; 11.5; 11.6; 11.18; 11.42; 11.43; 11.44; 11.45; 11.46; 11.47; 11.48; 12.1; 12.2; 12.4; 12.5; 12.6; 12.7; 12.8; 12.9; 12.10; 12.11; 12.12; 12.13; 14.2; 14.3; 14.4; 14.5; 14.8; 14.9; 14.10; 14.12; 14.13; 14.14; 14.15; 14.16; 14.17; 14.18; 14.19; 14.20; 14.21; 14.22; 14.23; 14.24; 14.25; 14.26; 14.27; 14.28; 14.29; p. 110 (1), p. 133 (12); p. 136, 137 (1–8); p. 139 (4, 5, 7–9); p. 140 (1–3); p. 148 (1); p. 149 (3, 4, 5); 151 (9); p. 154 (1); p. 155 (3–5, 8)
Minke, Stephanus: p. 139 (6)
Nakano, Katsura: p. 88, 89 (1–7)
Pelikan, Karin: p. 155 (6, 7)
Quedlinburger Architekturkonzepte: p. 138 (1, 2)
Scharmer, Dirk: 13.1
Scheicher, Georg: p. 128, 129 (1–8)
Shakti Haus (Körner, Schäberle): p. 90, 91 (1–7)
Six b design (Amy Jenkin): p. 112, 113 (1–7); p. 115 (10–13)
Six b design (Jamie Brennan): p. 114 (8, 9)
Smoothy, Paul: p. 120, 121 (1–7)
Steen et al. 1994: 8.3; 8.6
Sunlab Architecture with six b design: p. 148 (2); p. 150 (7)
The Last Straw: 2.9
The Salamander Company: p. 94, 95 (1–7)
Weber, Peter: 8.3
Wedig, Harald: 2.10
Welger: 3.4
Wanek, Catherine: p. 86, 87 (1–4)
Williams, Nick: p. 84, 85 (1–4)

About the authors

In 1974, Gernot Minke founded the Research Laboratory for Experimental Building (FEB) at the University of Kassel, devoted to the exploration of natural building materials. At this laboratory, he directed more than 40 research and development projects in the field of building with earth, building with straw, green roofs and low-cost housing. He taught at the University of Kassel for more than 35 years and participated in more than 60 international conferences. Minke is also an independent architect and worldwide advisor for building ecology as well as the author of numerous articles and several technical books, among them *Building with Earth* (2013) and *Building with Bamboo* (2016).

Benjamin Krick, born in 1976, studied architecture at the University of Applied Sciences Darmstadt and at the University of Kassel. His dissertation was in the field of experimental building with renewable materials. Since 2008, Krick has been a member of the Passivhaus Institut Darmstadt, where he heads a working group on component certification. He teaches at the University of Applied Science Darmstadt where his focus is on the energy-efficient building envelope as well as the sustainability assessment of the building's energy supply. As a lecturer and author of numerous specialist articles and books, he enthusiastically spreads knowledge about energy-efficient and sustainable buildings.

Subject index

Cover: Straw bale house "Mühlenhölzchen", Bad Belzig, Germany
(Design: Dirk Hottelmann; planning and construction: Timo Brenner)
Graphic design, layout and typesetting: Heike Strempel
Copy editing and project management: Ria Stein
Translation into English: Jörn Frenzel, Julian Reisenberger (chapters 6, 7, 9, 10, 13),
Ria Stein
Production: Heike Strempel
Paper: 135 g/m² Magno Volume
Lithography: Bildpunkt Druckvorstufen GmbH
Printing: optimal media GmbH

Originally published in German under the title of *Handbuch Strohballenbau: Grundlagen Konstruktionen Beispiele*
Copyright © 2014 ökobuch Verlag GmbH, Staufen bei Freiburg/Breisgau

For this English edition, the chapters were updated and new case studies were added.
Several chapters are loosely based on the publication by Gernot Minke and Friedemann Mahlke *Building with Straw. Design and Technology of a Sustainable Architecture*, published in 2005 by Birkhäuser Verlag.

Library of Congress Control Number: 2020936305
Bibliographic information published by the German National Library
The German National Library lists this publication in the Deutsche Nationalbibliografie;
detailed bibliographic data are available on the Internet at http://dnb.dnb.de.

ISBN 978-3-0356-1854-9
e-ISBN (PDF) 978-3-0356-1875-4

© 2020 Birkhäuser Verlag GmbH, Basel
P.O. Box 44, 4009 Basel, Switzerland
Part of Walter de Gruyter GmbH, Berlin/Boston

Printed on acid-free paper produced from chlorine-free pulp. TCF ∞
Printed in Germany

9 8 7 6 5 4 3 2 1

www.birkhauser.com